Differentiated Instruction for ESL Learners
With Student-Centered Projects

Toolkit for ESL Teachers

SUE HUBBERT
TARU NIEMINEN

Differentiated Instruction for ESL Learners

With Student-Centered Projects

Supplementary activities for

Levels I – III

Sue Hubbert, M.A. and Taru Nieminen, M.A.T.

Library of Congress Cataloging-in-Publication Data

Differentiated instruction for ESL learners with student-centered projects. /Sue Hubbert and Taru Nieminen

ISBN 978-0-9889791-5-4

1. English language— Study and teaching. 2. English as a Second Language— Study and teaching. 3. Foreign language-- Study and teaching. 4. Differentiated instruction. 5. Curriculum. 6. Assessment and rubrics.

Copyright ©2013 Hubbert and Nieminen

Edited by Sue Hubbert and Taru Nieminen

Layout and design by Taru Nieminen and Kristiina Gray

Cover Layout by Ashley Kasul

ISBN 978-0-9889791-5-4

The purchase of this book entitles the buyer to reproduce the activities and assessment rubric pages for classroom use only. All rights reserved. This book may not be reproduced, transmitted, or stored in whole or in part by any means, including graphic, electronic, or mechanical without the express written consent of the authors except in the case of brief quotations embodied in critical articles and reviews. For information regarding permission, please write to Sue Hubbert and Taru Nieminen via e-mail with the subject line of: **ESL Permissions** at WLToolkit@gmail.com.

At the time of publication, all websites and other factual content are the most current available. All URLs are accurate and active. The authors make no warranty or guarantee concerning the information and materials given out by organizations or content found at web sites. The authors are not responsible for any changes that occur after the publication of this book. If you find an error, please contact the authors at WLToolkit@gmail.com.

Our toolkit includes engaging, supplementary activities to foster critical thinking, creativity, responsibility, and independence in an ESL classroom.

- Teaching tips included with each section!

- Aligned to ACTFL Foreign Language and TESOL's PreK-12 English Language Proficiency Standards- each activity coded for easy transition into your lesson plans!

- An assessment rubric is provided with each activity sheet- grading is a snap!

- Each unit contains supplementary projects to create and nurture an exciting learning environment for your ESL learners!

We hope you and your students enjoy these lessons as much as we do!

Sincerely,

Sue Hubbert and Taru Nieminen

©2013 Hubbert and Nieminen

Table of Contents

Introduction

- The Why and the How 1
- Teacher Tips for Successful Projects 2
- Student Tips and Responsibilities 4
- Definitions and Abbreviations 5
- English Speaking Countries 6
- Measurement Equivalent Table 7
- ACTFL and TESOL Standards aligned to Assessment Rubrics 8

Unit 1: Getting Started

A

- Teacher Tips Page for Section A 10
- Alphabet 11
- Names and Nametags 13
- Numbers and Money 15
- Expressing Time 17

B

- Teacher Tips Page for Section B 19
- Dates, Days of the Week, and Months 20
- Seasons and Weather 22
- Greetings, Responses, and Introductions 24
- Colors and Clothing 26

C

- Teacher Tips Page for Section C 28
- Classroom Objects 29
- School Subjects, Teachers, and Times 31
- Family Nouns 33

Unit 2: Connecting with Culture

- ❖ *Teacher Tips for Pages 37 to 44* 36
- ❖ General Heritage and Customs 37
- ❖ Customs and Traditions 39
- ❖ Family Life 41
- ❖ Foods 43
- ❖ *Teacher Tips for Pages 46 to 53* 45
- ❖ Traditional Clothing 46
- ❖ Modern Clothing 48
- ❖ Arts and Education 50
- ❖ Famous People 52

Unit 3: Home and Abroad

- ❖ *Teacher Tips Page for Unit 3* 55
- ❖ House and Home 56
- ❖ Neighborhood and Directions 58
- ❖ City and Transportation 60

Unit 4: Body and Mind

- ❖ *Teacher Tips Page for Unit 4* 63
- ❖ Parts of the Body 64
- ❖ Sports and Hobbies 66
- ❖ Feelings and Emotions 68
- ❖ Technology 70

Unit 5: Score with Grammar

- Teacher Tips for Pages 74 to 81 73
- Nouns 74
- Adjectives 76
- Pronouns…. 78
- Verbs 80
- Teacher Tips for Pages 83 to 87 82
- Exclamations, Questions, and Declarative Sentences 83
- Likes and Dislikes 85

Unit 6: Going Places

- Teacher Tips for Pages 90 to 97 89
- Going to the Market 90
- Choose Your Ticket: Sporting Events, Concerts, Bus and Train Rides 92
- Vacation and Travel 94
- Visiting or Obtaining Services from Community Service Programs 96
- Teacher Tips for Pages 99 to 105 98
- Shopping Experience 99
- Eating Out 101
- Public and Private Schools 104

Reference Pages and Templates

- Teacher Tips for Pages 108-116 107
- Shopping List 108
- Facts and Figures 109
- Commands 110
- Clock template 111
- Facebook Page template 112
- Race for the Numbers 114
- Bingo Chart template 115
- More VERB activities 116

Introduction

❖ The Why and the How

Why?
- ❖ We need to produce leaders who are creative, critical, and independent thinkers
- ❖ Latest research reveals the effectiveness of Student-Centered teaching and Project-Based learning
- ❖ Differentiated Instruction allows each student to achieve his/her level of development and success
- ❖ Projects allow students to work at their own levels
- ❖ Ready-made assessments with rubrics support Common-Core Standards
- ❖ Student assignments are required to meet cross-curricular standards

This Book:
- ❖ Aligns to ACTFL Foreign Language and TESOL's PreK–12 English Language Proficiency Standards
- ❖ Fits into the Project-Based Learning format
- ❖ Challenges the unique learning styles of each student
- ❖ Encourages more mature language acquisition
- ❖ Offers many projects with cross-curricular standards
- ❖ Provides the learner with Student-Centered and Student-Generated projects

How?
- ❖ Teachers give the students the suggestion of an *idea* which sparks critical and innovative thinking instead of word-for-word instruction
- ❖ The students' determination of *how* to use the information is crucial to the creation of the leaders and innovators of the next generation
- ❖ The projects keep all work student centered and student generated
- ❖ Students are empowered when given the reins to direct their own learning
- ❖ Teachers can easily recognize the connection between the activity and the Proficiency Standard it supports

This Book:
- ❖ Facilitates the inclusion of standards into the teachers' lesson plans
- ❖ Provides teacher tips for activities which spark critical and innovative thinking
- ❖ Generates independent thinkers
- ❖ Allows students to make integral decisions to achieve project success
- ❖ Builds on the general principles of Second Language Acquisition and independent study
- ❖ Provides different language situations through realistic interactions

❖ Teacher Tips for Successful Projects

- ❖ Have students use English as much as possible to complete projects.
- ❖ Although not included in each assessment, it is expected that students use correct grammar and spelling for all projects.
- ❖ To effectively use English, most projects have a requirement for a presentation element to class or teacher. Adjustments may be necessary to achieve the desired student outcome.
- ❖ If you have time constraints to showcase student projects, split students into groups and have each student within a group present his/her project. This enables you to go around the room to listen, watch, and assess.
- ❖ Displaying and presenting projects gives students a sense of accomplishment and pride.
- ❖ When students complete "Your Choice" projects, it is their responsibility to write down assessment requirements for your approval. Students should write these in the rubric square provided. It may be necessary for you to give additional help when students are writing assessment requirements.
- ❖ Unless otherwise noted, students are expected to use color in all the projects. There are only a few exceptions. Research has proven that COLOR stimulates and inspires creativity! ☺
- ❖ In the projects, students should be as close to scale as possible, should use appropriate size within the project, i.e. all elements must correspond in size and distance.
- ❖ Because of the creative nature of the projects, please ensure that students understand the *required* elements of the projects.
- ❖ Since every teacher, classroom, and group of students are unique, please feel free to add or remove any elements of the assessments to adapt to your particular situation.
- ❖ **Menus:**
    - o **Tic-tac-toe**: Students choose 3 in a row; diagonal, across or down.
    - o **Nine-Square Menu**: Students choose two to complete.
    - o **Columns**: Students complete one from Column I and one more from Columns II or III.
    - o **Score 100**: Instructions are on the project sheet.
    - o **List menu**: Instructions are on the project sheet.
- ❖ **Teacher's Choice Projects:**
    - o Excellent group projects.
    - o Teacher chooses groups.
    - o Teacher assigns project(s) for each group.
    - o Teacher gives groups a time limit on presentation.
    - o Group presents its project together; all members must be part of presentation.
    - o Projects make great displays for the classroom.
    - o OPTIONAL: Have each group come up with 2-3 questions about their topic which the teacher then transfers onto a worksheet for students to complete as a quiz.
    - o TECHNOLOGY IS FABULOUS: Teachers have students email the questions to them which the teachers then proofread, copy, and paste to a document: quiz created. ☺
- ❖ **Easy Grading for *Score 100* menu**:

> This menu requires students to select one or more projects which add up to 100. To keep the assessment simple, the rubrics use the same point value (25) as all others. To calculate final grade for each student, determine the percentage of points earned.
>
> **EXAMPLE 1**: Student A has chosen the 20, 30, and 50 *Score 100*-projects from the menu. Student A has received 60 out of 75 on the assessment rubrics. To determine overall percentage, divide 60 by 75. The student has earned an 80% for a grade.
>
> **EXAMPLE 2**: Student B has chosen the 20 and 80 *Score 100*-projects and has received a total of 45 out of 50 on the assessment rubrics. Divide 45 by 50; student has earned a 90% for a grade.

- **How to define *creativity* as an assessment?** In some projects, we have included "Creativity counts" as an assessment piece. Below are the dictionary definitions for the words *creative, original,* and *imagination*.
    - *Creative*: 1. Characterized by originality; 2. Imaginative.
    - *Original*: 1. Initial, first; 2. Fresh and unusual, new; 3. Creative, inventive.
    - *Imagination*: 1. The process or power of forming a mental image of something not real or present; 2. Creativity, inventiveness; 3. Resourcefulness.
- ❖ **Take something that is known, and give it a fresh approach, as in the following examples:**
    - A kite is designed to hang in the room. One girl's kite is a tuxedo. A boy's kite is shaped like a basketball.
    - A game is created with a painted pizza box as a game board and container "all in one."
    - A PowerPoint is designed with a fresh approach to share the information. E.g. music, animation, or graphics are innovatively added.
    - A song is composed with original lyrics and score.
- ❖ **Challenges**
    - Use as additional individual projects or as extra credit projects.
- ❖ **We recommend you have the following items on hand in order to complete most of the projects:**
    - Poster board, glue, glue gun, tape, markers, colored pencils, white copy paper, 9 x 12 in. and 12 x 18 in. construction paper, scissors, old magazines of all kinds, magazines in English, yarn, string, paper fasteners/brads, paper punch, rulers.
    - Shopping list of items provided in the *Reference Pages and Templates* section.

- ❖ **How to bind books:**
    - Staple the sheets of paper down the middle of the book with an oversized book stapler.
    - Paper-punch holes (min. 2 required) in the side of the book and lace them together.
    - Paper-punch and use individual rings, bag ties, wire, etc. to tie the book together.
    - Fold and staple along the spine (min. 2 staples).
    - Sew along spine with sewing machine or use yarn.
    - Use brass fasteners to keep book together.
    - Make sure that sharp ends of staples are covered with tape or glue.
- ❖ **How to make flipbooks:**

    Here are a few websites we found:
    - http://www.readwritethink.org/files/resources/interactives/flipbook/ (You are able to type the titles, draw, type text onto the pages, and print the book!)
    - http://pinterest.com/sjww/teacher-made-books/ (Many types of different books to make.)
    - YouTube videos: https://www.youtube.com/watch?v=4N0X3DkXNtM and https://www.youtube.com/watch?v=S824yY9ZeqM.
- ❖ **Check out our website for some examples of completed student projects:**
    http://wltoolkit.com/student-work/

❖ Student Instructions for Successful Projects

- ❖ The purpose is to connect you with the English language.
- ❖ Use English to complete projects.
- ❖ Although not included in each assessment, it is required that you use correct grammar and spelling for all projects.
- ❖ Remember that your teacher is an important resource when writing the necessary project requirements for "Your Choice". (Hint: Write the items first on a separate sheet, so your teacher can make changes and then write the items on the rubric sheet.)
- ❖ Remember to keep a copy of the rubric so the teacher can use it to grade your project(s).
- ❖ The abbreviation *min.* means *minimum*: the smallest amount or size that is necessary for the project.
- ❖ The abbreviation *max.* means *maximum*: the largest amount or size that is necessary for the project.
- ❖ All illustrations should be in color. To do this, use markers, colored pencils, paints, magazine pictures, photos, pictures from the internet, and/or clipart.
- ❖ Since every teacher, classroom, and student is unique, please understand that your teacher may change any item of the assessment rubric.
- ❖ Keep a journal to write down ideas for future projects.
- ❖ **Here are some things you can start to collect for future projects:**
    - o Shoeboxes and other boxes that are the correct size for dioramas
    - o Poster board, large pieces of cardboard
    - o Scrapbook materials
    - o Old magazines

- ❖ **How to bind books:**
    - o Staple the sheets of paper down the middle of the book with an oversized book stapler.
    - o Paper-punch holes (min. 2 required) in the side of the book and tie them together.
    - o Paper-punch and use individual rings, bag ties, wire, etc. to tie the book together.
    - o Fold and staple along the spine (min. 2 staples).
    - o Sew along spine with a sewing machine or use yarn.
    - o Use brass fasteners to keep the book together.
    - o Make sure that sharp ends of staples are covered with tape or glue.
- ❖ **Interesting Facts about Language**
    - o Korean is the only language which has a known origin.
    - o Chinese, Japanese, and Finnish are the three hardest languages to learn in the world. They compete for first place amongst each other in most polls taken.
    - o English: What other words besides "hungry" and "angry" end in "-gry?" There aren't any!
    - o The United Nations uses six official languages to conduct business: English, French, Spanish, Chinese, Russian and Arabic.[1]
    - o It's estimated that up to 7,000 different languages are spoken around the world.[2]
    - o Eskimoes have hundreds of words for "ice" but none for "hello."[3]
    - o In nearly every language around the world, the word for "mother" begins with an *m* sound. Some exceptions can be found in the Uralic language group (e.g. äiti in Finnish.)[4]

---

[1] http://www.bbc.co.uk/languages/guide/languages.shtml
[2] http://www.bbc.co.uk/languages/guide/languages.shtml
[3] http://www.rcasteel.com/StrangeThings/language.aspx
[4] http://www.allfunandgames.ca/facts/languages.shtml

❖ Definitions

- <u>Acrostic:</u> A poem or series of lines in which certain letters, such as the first in a line or verse, form a name, motto, or message when read in order. Examples:

Language study	**C**aring
Entertains	**O**ver-the-top
All who	**R**ambunctious
Respond	**A**gile
Nicely	

- <u>Approve:</u> To accept, permit, or agree
- <u>Assessment rubric:</u> A scoring scale used to evaluate student performance for a task-specific set of criteria
- <u>Bibliography:</u> A list of the works of an author or of sources of information in print or online on a specific subject
- <u>Brochure:</u> A pamphlet or a booklet that is often used for advertisement or information
- <u>Format:</u> The number and size of spaces in a record or graph, or the spacing and punctuation of information in a written report or graph
- <u>Decorate:</u> To improve and enhance the appearance of your project with color and design
- <u>Diorama:</u> A three-dimensional miniature scene with painted, molded figures and background
- <u>Flipbook:</u> A set of sheets of paper, hinged so that they can be flipped over to show information or illustrations in sequence
- <u>Illustrate:</u> To explain or decorate a text with pictures, photographs, or diagrams
- <u>Mobile:</u> A hanging sculpture consisting of parts that move
- <u>Scrapbook:</u> A book with blank pages for mounting pictures and other mementoes
- <u>Skit:</u> A short, usually comical, theatrical play/drama

❖ Abbreviations

- E.g. = For example
- I.e. (i.e.) = In other words
- Etc. = et cetera = and so on
- Min. = Minimum
  The abbreviation *min.* means *minimum*: the smallest amount or size that is necessary for the project.
- Max. = Maximum
  The abbreviation *max.* means *maximum*: the largest amount or size that is necessary for the project.

❖ English-speaking countries

We consider the following countries to be English speaking countries. All of them are suitable for use with the projects and activities in our book.

- Australia*
- Canada
- Ireland
- New Zealand
- England*
- United States of America

  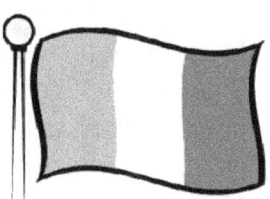

*Official names for Australia and England:

Australia = Commonwealth of Australia

England = The United Kingdom of Great Britain and Northern Ireland

Differentiated Instruction for ESL Learners

Measurement Equivalent Table

Item	Inches	Centimeters
Standard poster	27 x 41	~ 68 x 104
Shoebox	Approx. 5 W x 4 H x 16 L	~ 13 W x 10 H x 40 L
Letter size paper	8.5 x 11	A 4 = 21 x 29.7
3 x 5 in. index cards	3 x 5	~ 8 x 13
4 x 6 in. index card	4 x 6	~ 10 x 15
Construction paper	9 x 12 / 12 x 18	~23 x 30 / 30 x 45
Half-sheet	5.5 x 8.5	~14 x 20
Timeline	3 ft. long, 1 ft. high	~90 x 30

Great site for converting measurement of all kinds!

❖ http://www.worldwidemetric.com/measurements.html

❖ National Standards for Foreign Language Learning (U.S.)

Each project has been tagged with one of the national standards; however, many of the projects meet more than one national standard when completed by the student. Many projects also meet various cross-curricular standards.

- ❖ **STANDARDS FOR FOREIGN LANGUAGE LEARNING** can be found on the American Council on the Teaching of Foreign Languages website: http://www.actfl.org/ and further in their publication: National Standards for Foreign Language Education.

❖ TESOL PreK-12 English Language Proficiency Standards

Each project has also been tagged with one of the TESOL standards; however, some of the projects meet more than one TESOL standard when completed by the student. Many projects also meet various cross-curricular standards. One of the four language domains (listening, speaking, reading, and writing) has been included with each standard.

- ❖ **PROFICIENCY STANDARDS FOR TESOL** can be found on the Teachers of English to Speakers of Other Languages website: http://tesol.org and further in their publication: TESOL PreK-12 English Language Proficiency Standards.

Language Domains:
Listening = L   Speaking = S   Reading = R   Writing = W

- ❖ **ASSESSMENT**

  Based on the National Foreign Language Learning and TESOL Standards

  - The "Teacher Tips" pages for each section or unit contain the National Foreign Language Learning and TESOL Standard for each of the student projects. (TESOL standard with language domain(s) is **BOLDED**)

  - The format of the National Foreign Language Learning and TESOL Standards diagram corresponds to the assessment rubric format for each project sheet. Example below.

Alphabet Assessment Rubric

*Write an Acrostic Poem __/5	*Make Flashcards __/5	*Create Word Search __/5
*Lead a Spelling Bee __/5	*Your Choice! __/5	*Design a Game __/5
*Write an Alphabet Book __/5	*Draw an Alphabet People Poster __/5	*Compose a Song or a Rap __/5

Corresponding ACTFL and TESOL Standards

Alphabet		
1.2 – **2L**	1.2 – **2L**	1.2 – **2W**
1.2 – **2R**		1.3 – **2R**
1.3 – **2R**	3.1 – **2R** +Art	1.3 – **2R**

Unit 1: Getting Started

A
- Teacher Tips Page for Section A 10
- Alphabet 11
- Names and Nametags 13
- Numbers and Money 15
- Expressing Time 17

B
- Teacher Tips Page for Section B 19
- Dates, Days of the Week, and Months 20
- Seasons and Weather 22
- Greetings, Responses, and Introductions 24
- Colors and Clothing 26

C
- Teacher Tips Page for Section C 28
- Classroom Objects 29
- School Subjects, Teachers, and Times 31
- Family Nouns 33

Teacher Tips Page for Section A

Standards

Alphabet

1.2 – 2W	1.2 – 2W	1.2 – 2W
1.2 – 2S		1.3 – 2W
1.3 – 2W	3.1 – 2W +Art	1.3 – 2SW

- Challenge: 1.1 – 2S

Names and Nametags

All projects
3.2 – 1SW

Numbers and Money

2.2 – 3W	1.3 – 3W	1.3 – 3W
3.1 – 2S		3.1 – 2W +Math
1.3 – 2SW	4.1 – 2W	1.3 – 2W

Time

1.1 – 1W	1.3 – 1W	4.2 – 1W
1.3 – 1W		4.1 – 2W +Tech
1.2 – 2W	1.3 – 2W	2.1 – 2W

- Challenge: 1.1 – 2S

- ❖ **Preview Material**
  - o For videotaped or recorded products, it is always wise to preview the video or recording prior to class presentation.
- ❖ **Alphabet**
  - o Example for an Alphabet Acrostic in English:
    - **A**ffirming
    - **L**iterate
    - **P**ractical
    - **H**ip and happening
    - **A**ccurate
    - **B**eautiful
    - **E**ntertaining
    - **T**errific
- ❖ **Numbers and Money**
  - o For easy conversion tables and a universal currency converter, use http://www.xe.com/.
- ❖ **Time**
  - o Make copies of Facebook Page template on page 112-113.

The Alphabet

Select "Three-in-a-Row" to complete the tic-tac-toe.

Write an Acrostic Poem	Make Flashcards	Make a Word Search
Write an acrostic poem for the word *alphabet* in English using vocabulary words.	Draw a picture of each letter of the English alphabet. May be completed with a partner.	Make a word search with every letter of the alphabet in English.
Lead a Spelling Bee	Your Choice!	Make a Game
Use vocabulary words or student names in English to lead a spelling bee for your classmates. 		Design a game using the alphabet in English.
Write an Alphabet Book	Make an Alphabet People Poster	Write and Sing a Song or a Rap
Write and illustrate an alphabet book in English.	Draw the "Alphabet People" and use vocabulary words. 	Write and sing an original song or rap using the alphabet.

➢ **Challenge**: Shoot a Video of yourself teaching and/or learning the alphabet in English.

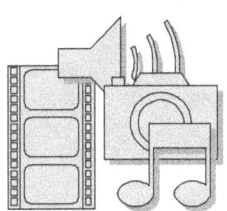

Shoot a Video	
* Must include all letters of the English alphabet	___ / 5
* Clear pronunciation and good volume	___ / 5
* Use a min. of 5 visuals or props	___ / 5
* Give a tape to the teacher to watch before the performance	___ / 5
* Perform live or play video for the class	___ / 5
Total points	___ / 25

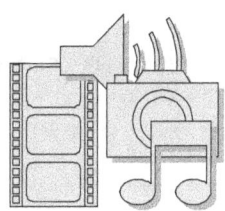

Alphabet Assessment Rubric

Write an Acrostic Poem		Make Flashcards		Make a Word Search	
* Min. 8.5 x 11 in. paper	____/5	* Max. 4 x 6 in. index card	____/5	* Min. 8.5 x 11 in. paper	____/5
* Each word or phrase must begin with one of the letters of the word *alphabet*	____/5	* Must have an item which begins with the same letter that is on the card	____/5	* Must have a min. of 20 vocabulary words	____/5
* Typed or neatly written with the word *alphabet* printed from top to bottom on the left side of the paper	____/5	* Write the name of each item on the other side of the card; use correct spelling	____/5	* Each word must start with a different letter of the alphabet	____/5
* Use color	____/5	* Cards must be in a container or bag	____/5	* Include answer key and puzzle	____/5
* Illustrate your poem	____/5	* Present to class	____/5	* Neatly written or typed	____/5
Total points	____/25	**Total points**	____/25	**Total Points**	____/25
Lead a Spelling Bee		_____!		Make a Game	
* Use a min. of 20 words or names	____/5		____/5	* Must include 20 questions or activity cards	____/5
* Write each word or name on a half-sheet of paper	____/5		____/5	* Give your game a name	____/5
* Print words neatly	____/5		____/5	* Write a set of rules	____/5
* Make a certificate for the winner(s)	____/5		____/5	* Make a written plan for choosing teams and the playing order	____/5
* Lead the spelling bee	____/5		____/5	* Play the game with the class	____/5
Total points	____/25	**Total points**	____/25	**Total points**	____/25
Write an Alphabet Book		Make an Alphabet People Poster		Write and Sing a Song or Rap	
* Min. 5.5 x 8.5 in. bound book	____/5	* Standard poster size	____/5	* Sing live or play video	____/5
* Illustrate the front and the back covers	____/5	* Draw each letter with different alphabet people	____/5	* Include each letter of the English alphabet	____/5
* Include every letter of the alphabet	____/5	* Must use vocabulary words	____/5	* Must have melody	____/5
* Illustrate in color	____/5	* Must be in color	____/5	* Must be sung in alphabetical order	____/5
* Write your English name on the front cover	____/5	* Write your English name on the back of the poster	____/5	* Give taped or written copy of words to teacher to read before singing	____/5
Total points	____/25	**Total points**	____/25	**Total points**	____/25

Show your project choices to your teacher by: _____

All of your projects are due on: _____

Names and Nametags

A complete language experience calls for the student to immerse herself in the English language. There is no better way than to require the students to pick an English first name for themselves. This should be accomplished within the first week of the class, preferably in the first three days. Doing this has proven to be very effective for student involvement.

How to make nametags:

- **Items needed:**
    - Poster board or heavy cardboard
    - Markers, pens, pencils, colored pencils
    - String/yarn
- **Directions:**
    - Cut the board to about 4 x 11 in. size (this is big enough to see from across the room, as students need to learn each other's names!)
    - Students write their new first names onto cardboard and illustrate with pictures that tell about them.

Activities for students/teacher to learn new names:

- Introduce oneself in English.
- "My name is…" game. Items needed: nametags and a ball or other soft object to throw.
    - Say "My name is…" in English, then…
    - Say someone else's name and toss the ball to that person.
    - The person to whom you throw the ball says "My name is…." and so on.
    - It is important that the ball reaches everyone in the room: a student may not toss the ball to someone who has already had a turn.
- Same activity as the "My name is…" game, but the ball always gets passed to the person on the right. This is a faster version if you are pressed for time or just need a quick activity for an end or start of the class.
- Teacher instructs students to whom to throw the ball. Great activity for the teacher to learn the students' new names.
- After the 2nd day with nametags, have students flip their nametags (or put them away) for the last couple of rounds of any of the games, and then start the "My name is…." game.
- Spelling Bee with student names. Each correctly spelled name receives a point/ reward.
- Students write names on the board. Teacher gives points to each correctly spelled name.
- **Name Quiz:**
    - Students sit in their desks.
    - Each student has a large number on a piece of paper fastened to the front of his/her desk.
    - Give each student a "quiz" paper with number of students in class, e.g. 1-25.
    - Students write each student's name on corresponding line.

OR

- Teacher provides a list of names to match or to rewrite names on the line.

Nametag Assessment Rubric

Make a Nametag	
* About 4 x 11 in.	____/5
* Use heavy paper or cardboard	____/5
* Spell name correctly	____/5
* Must use color	____/5
* Name can be read from across the room	____/5
Total points	____/ 25

Handmade

Computer-made

Numbers and Money

Select "Three-in-a-Row" to complete the tic-tac-toe.

Make a List	Make a Game	Make a Picture Book
Make a list of at least 10 items in your room at home using English monetary units.	Make a game with numbers using English.	Design a picture book of numbers with pictures and labels.
Do a Cheer	Your Choice!	Create a Worksheet
Plan and do a cheer. You may make a video to show your talent. 		Make a worksheet using the numbers 1-100. 
Draw a Poster	Make Flashcards	Make a Crossword Puzzle
Draw a poster with at least 10 items labeled with a price in English monetary units. Call on classmates to express the cost in English.	Make flashcards with the written number word in English on one side and the numeral on the other side.	Create a crossword puzzle to solve number problems. Answers to problems must be in English and must be written out.

Numbers and Money Assessment Rubric

Make a List		Make a Game		Make a Picture Book	
* Include a min. of 10 items	___/5	* Include a min. of 20 question or activity cards	___/5	* Min. 5.5 x 8.5 in. bound book	___/5
* Illustrate in color or cut pictures from magazines	___/5	* Give your game a name	___/5	* Use a min. of 10 pages and a min. 25 numbers	___/5
* Each item must have a price tag	___/5	* Make a written plan for choosing teams and the playing order	___/5	* Illustrate in color (drawings, magazine or internet pictures)	___/5
* Write the name of each item next to the picture	___/5	* Write a set of rules	___/5	* Label each picture	___/5
* Present to the class	___/5	* Play the game with the class	___/5	* Read your book to the class	___/5
Total points	___/25	**Total points**	___/25	**Total Points**	___/25

Do a Cheer		_____!		Create a Worksheet	
* Min. 1 minute long	___/5		___/5	* Typed or neatly written	___/5
* Include 20 target items	___/5		___/5	* Must have addition and subtraction problems	___/5
* Record cheer for teacher to listen to before performing	___/5		___/5	* Use numbers from 1-100	___/5
* Ask a friend to do the cheer with you	___/5		___/5	* Answer must be 100 or less	___/5
* Perform live or play video	___/5		___/5	* Include answer key	___/5
Total points	___/25	**Total points**	___/25	**Total points**	___/25

Draw a Poster		Make Flashcards		Make a Crossword Puzzle	
* Standard poster size	___/5	* 3 x 5 in. index cards	___/5	* Include a min. of 20 clues	___/5
* Include a min. of 10 items labeled with names	___/5	* Use a min. of 25 cards with container or bag	___/5	* Write clues using numerals	___/5
* Each item must have a price tag	___/5	* Answer must be 100 or less	___/5	* Write the answer in English	___/5
* Call on classmates to say the cost in English	___/5	* Write the number problem on one side and the answer on the other side	___/5	* 3 classmates must solve puzzle (turn in completed and corrected puzzles)**	___/5
* Illustrate in color (drawings, magazine or internet pictures)	___/5	* Play the game with a partner	___/5	* Give original puzzle and answer key to the teacher	___/5
Total points	___/25	**Total points**	___/25	**Total points**	___/25

Show your project choices to your teacher by: _____

All of your projects are due on: _____

**Ask teacher to make copies.

Differentiated Instruction for ESL Learners ©2013 Hubbert and Nieminen

Expressing Time

Select "Three-in-a-Row" to complete the tic-tac-toe.

Make Flashcards	Make a Poster	Create a Flipbook
Make flashcards with the clock on one side and the correct phrase in English on the other side.	Design a large clock poster to illustrate and teach the time expressions in English.	Make a flipbook with clock faces on the front and the correct times in English on the inside.
Make a Picture Book	Your Choice! 	Update Facebook
Write and draw a picture book with illustrations telling what the characters do at different times during the day.		"Update" your page telling your friends about your plans on Saturday. You are very busy! List 10 activities and the times using English.
Write a Diary Entry	Perform a Dialogue	Make an Airline Schedule
Tell your diary about your daily schedule at school: what you do (classes and activities) and at what time you do them.	Write a dialogue in English telling the times of different activities. Perform the dialogue with a classmate.	Make an airline schedule on a large poster showing the arrivals and departures of different flights in an English speaking country.

➢ **Challenge**: <u>Create a Schedule</u> of your family activities for an entire week.

Create a Schedule	
* Use time expressions in English	____ / 5
* Min. 2 entries per day for one week	____ / 5
* Neatly written schedule	____ / 5
* Use color and pictures	____ / 5
* Present to class in a creative way	____ / 5
Total points	____ / 25

Expressing Time Assessment Rubric

Make Flashcards		Make a Poster		Create a Flipbook	
* 3 x 5 in. index cards	___/5	* Standard poster size, use both sides of the poster	___/5	* Min. 8.5 x 11 in., folded in half	___/5
* Use a min. of 20 different expressions of time	___/5	* Use a min. of 20 different expressions of time	___/5	* Include 10 expressions of time	___/5
* Draw clock on one side, write correct phrase in English on the other side	___/5	* Clocks can be drawn, made from cut-outs, or computer generated	___/5	* Times must be in correct form in English	___/5
* Include container or bag for cards	___/5	* Pictures must be in color	___/5	* Illustrate in color	___/5
* Play the game with a partner	___/5	* Teach to the class	___/5	* Neatly written and drawn or computer generated	___/5
Total points	___/25	**Total points**	___/25	**Total Points**	___/25

Make a Picture Book		_____!		Update Facebook	
* Min. 5.5 x 8.5 in., bound book	___/5		___/5	* Use Facebook template	___/5
* Include a min. of 10 pages	___/5		___/5	* Include 10 activities using complete sentences	___/5
* Write title and student name on the cover	___/5		___/5	* All entries must be in English	___/5
* Use complete sentences in English	___/5		___/5	* Give copy of printed page to teacher to read	___/5
* Illustrations in color (drawings, magazine or internet pictures)	___/5		___/5	* Present to the class	___/5
Total points	___/25	**Total points**	___/25	**Total points**	___/25

Write a Diary Entry		Perform a Dialogue		Make an Airline Schedule	
* Include a min. of 10 entries of activities or classes	___/5	* Neatly written or typed; one copy for you, one for teacher to read	___/5	* Neatly written or typed	___/5
* Include a min. of 10 time expressions	___/5	* Use correct grammar and time expressions	___/5	* Include min. 5 arrivals and 5 departures	___/5
* Give your entries a title	___/5	* Min. 10 lines using complete sentences	___/5	* Use real city names	___/5
* Use the 1st person for all entries	___/5	* Use a min. of 5 different time expressions	___/5	* Include two out-of-country flights	___/5
* Neatly written or typed	___/5	* Perform for the class	___/5	* Must be in color	___/5
Total points	___/25	**Total points**	___/25	**Total points**	___/25

Show your project choices to your teacher by: _____

All of your projects are due on: _____

Teacher Tips Page for Section B

Standards

Expressing Dates, Days of the Week, and Months

1.3 – 1W	1.1 – 2L	1.3 – 4W
4.2 – 1W		1.3 - 2R
1.3 – 2LS	3.1 - 2RW +Art	1.1 – 2S

> Challenge 1: 4.1 – 2W

Seasons and Weather

3.1 – 4S +Science	2.1 – 4W	3.2 – 4W
3.2 – 4W		4.1 – 2W
4.1 – 2W	3.1 – 2W +Science	1.3 – 4R

> Challenge: 3.1 – 4SL +Science

Greetings, Responses and Introductions

All projects		
1.1 – 1LS	1.2 – 2SW	1.3 - 2R

Colors and Clothing

1.3 – 2W	1.1 – 2SW	3.1 – 1LS +Music
1.1 – 2LS		3.1 – 2SW +Tech
1.1 – 2S	1.1 – 2LS	1.2 – 2SW

> Challenge 1: 3.1 – 2W
> Challenge 2: 3.2 – 2W

❖ **Preview Material**
  o For videotaped or recorded products, it is always wise to preview the video or recording prior to class presentation.

❖ **Expressing Dates, Days of the Week, and Months**
  o Ideas for "Your Choice": Design T-shirts or socks for each day of the week or months of the year, draw a comic strip of goofy activities for each day of the week or each month of the year.

❖ Use **Greetings, Responses, and Introductions** assessment for a test! ☺

❖ **Colors and Clothing**
  o Give bonus points for "creative" thinkers, e.g. using target country fashions in projects.

❖ **Seasons and Weather**
  > **Extra Challenge:** Construct a Diorama. Build and label a diorama of the four seasons (or your favorite season) in an English speaking country. Write a paragraph in English describing your diorama. **Challenge:** 1.3 - **2W**

Construct a Diorama	
* Min. 1 shoebox size (or approx. 5x14x16 in.)	____ / 5
* Min. five 3-D objects	____ / 5
* Decorate all surfaces	____ / 5
* Name your diorama	____ / 5
* Write a paragraph with 3-6 sentences	____ / 5
Total points	____ / 25

Dates, Days of the Week, Months of the Year

Select "Three-in-a-Row" to complete the tic-tac-toe.

Make a Photo-folio	Make a Survey Chart	Design a Poster
Illustrate two activities for each day of the week using English. 	Make a survey chart with classmate birthdays. You need to interview each classmate to get your information.	Make a poster with the four seasons. Draw or use magazine or online photos. Include every month for each season.
Make a Calendar	**Your Choice!** 	**Make a Word Search**
Design a calendar in English for the next year with pictures for each month.		Create a word search using the days of the week and months of the year vocabulary.
List Family Birthdays	**Create a Craft Activity**	**Create a Timeline**
Tell the birthdays of your immediate family and good friends to the class.	Make a craft activity using target vocabulary.	Make a timeline of your family's important events during one calendar year. Can be in 3-D. 

➢ **Challenge:** Make a Children's Book using the song "Monday is the day we wash our clothes…" as you use English vocabulary.

Make a Children's Book	
* Min. 5.5 x 8.5 in., bound book	____ / 5
* Two activities for each day of the week	____ / 5
* Write a sentence to describe each activity	____ / 5
* Label each day of the week clearly	____ / 5
* Draw in color (may be stick figures)	____ / 5
Total points	____ / 25

Differentiated Instruction for ESL Learners ©2013 Hubbert and Nieminen

Dates, Days, Months of the Year Assessment Rubric

Make a Photo-folio		Make a Survey Chart		Design a Poster	
* Min. 5.5 x 8.5 in., bound book	___/5	* Ask a min. of 12 people	___/5	* Standard poster size	___/5
* Include two activities per day	___/5	* Write interview questions and answers in English	___/5	* Pictures in color (drawings, magazine or internet pictures)	___/5
* Write a sentence to describe each activity	___/5	* Make the chart by months; include all 12 months	___/5	* Label months and seasons clearly	___/5
* Label each day of the week clearly	___/5	* Illustrate in color	___/5	* Give your poster a name	___/5
* Draw in color (may be stick figures)	___/5	* Share results with the class using English	___/5	* Must be neat and readable with correct spelling	___/5
Total points	___/25	**Total points**	___/25	**Total Points**	___/25

Make a Calendar		_____!		Make a Word Search	
* Neatly written or computer generated with correct spelling	___/5		___/5	* Neatly written or typed	___/5
* Include all the months of the year and days of the week	___/5		___/5	* Include all days of the week and months of the year	___/5
* Must include major holidays of an English speaking country	___/5		___/5	* Have three classmates solve the puzzle and turn in corrected puzzles **	___/5
* Illustrate in color	___/5		___/5	* Include pictures and color in the word search	___/5
* Make the calendar for the next year	___/5		___/5	* Give puzzle and answer key to teacher	___/5
Total points	___/25	**Total points**	___/25	**Total points**	___/25

List Family Birthdays		Create a Craft Activity		Create a Timeline	
* Neatly written or typed in English	___/5	* Neatly written or typed	___/5	* No larger than 3 ft. long, 1 ft. high	___/5
* Include a min. of 10 family members	___/5	* Name your craft activity, and include a picture of the craft item	___/5	* Min. 12 events on the calendar with a brief description for each event	___/5
* Identify each member of the family, e.g. father, aunt, sister, mother	___/5	* Make a complete instruction sheet with drawings	___/5	* Write the dates in English	___/5
* Include drawing or photo of each person in color	___/5	* Have a classmate use your instruction sheet as he or she makes the craft	___/5	* Must include a colored drawing or 3-D object next to each date or event	___/5
* Present to the class	___/5	* Make the craft to show as an example	___/5	* Present to the class	___/5
Total points	___/25	**Total points**	___/25	**Total points**	___/25

Show your project choices to your teacher by: _____

All of your projects are due on: _____

**Ask your teacher to make copies.

Seasons and Weather

Select two projects to complete.

Build a Mobile	Make a Flipbook	Design a Brochure
Make a mobile of the four seasons in an English speaking country. Include descriptions of the seasons. 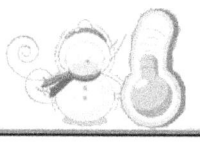	Make a flipbook of seasonal activities for an English speaking country. Inside each flap, draw and label at least two activities for the season using target vocabulary.	Make a colorful brochure for a resort in an English speaking country. Include seasonal and weather information for the resort area.
Create a Poster	 Your Choice!	Write an Acrostic Poem
Make a poster with the four seasons and the type of weather that an English speaking country would have during each season.		Write an acrostic poem for at least two seasons using adjectives in English.
Make a Venn Diagram	Research and Draw	Create a Card Game
Compare and contrast seasons and/or weather in an English speaking country with your native country. Compare, for example: clothing, temperatures, activities, weather, etc.	Research the types of weather* in an English speaking country. Draw the types of weather and use English terms to label each picture. *For example: tornado, flood, monsoon, hail storm, thunderstorm, rain, snow.	Make a card game with seasons and weather terms in English. 

➢ **Challenge:** <u>Research Different Weather Terms.</u> Draw and label the weather terms in English. Choose the way you will present them. Write 1-3 sentences describing each weather term.

Research Weather Terms	
* Labels must be in English	___/ 5
* Drawings must be in color	___/ 5
* List the places where you found the information	___/ 5
* Write 1-3 sentences in English	___/ 5
* Present to class in a creative way	___/ 5
Total points	___/ 25

22

Differentiated Instruction for ESL Learners   ©2013 Hubbert and Nieminen

Seasons and Weather Assessment Rubric

Build a Mobile		Make a Flipbook		Design a Brochure	
* Include a min. of 10 pieces of written information in English	/5	* Min. 8.5 x 11 in. paper, folded	/5	* Min. 8.5 x 11 in. paper, folded	/5
* Illustrations must be in color	/5	* Write the name of the season on front flap	/5	* Include seasonal and weather information	/5
* Mobile must have 3 levels	/5	* Include and label all four seasons	/5	* Must have both pictures and written information	/5
* Must be balanced; i.e. must hang evenly	/5	* Label two seasonal activities for each season under each flap	/5	* Neatly written or computer generated	/5
* Show and tell to the class	/5	* Illustrate in color	/5	* Creativity counts	/5
Total points	/25	**Total points**	/25	**Total Points**	/25

Create a Poster		_____!		Write an Acrostic Poem	
* Standard poster size	/5		/5	* Min. 8.5 x 11 in.	/5
* Illustrations in color (drawings, magazine or internet pictures)	/5		/5	* Neatly written or typed with word lined up on the left side of the paper	/5
* Write a description for the weather and label the seasons	/5		/5	* Words must be adjectives and must be in English	/5
* Use English	/5		/5	* Illustrate your poem in color	/5
* Include name of English speaking country in the title	/5		/5	* Display in class	/5
Total points	/25	**Total points**	/25	**Total points**	/25

Make a Venn Diagram		Research and Draw		Create a Card Game	
* Min. 8.5 x 11 in. paper	/5	* Include research on a separate page (bibliography)	/5	* Cards are 3 x 5 in. size	/5
* Name each part of the diagram and give your Venn a name	/5	* Illustrations in color	/5	* Make a min. of 10-20 cards or amount necessary to play the game	/5
* Must be neatly drawn	/5	* Include weather zone map for the target country	/5	* Decorate one side of each card with picture(s) and with name of the game	/5
* Use a min. of 12 items in English	/5	* Label the pictures	/5	* Type instructions on "how to play"	/5
* Make your Venn Diagram colorful	/5	* Use a poster or brochure to display your research	/5	* Include container or bag for cards	/5
Total points	/25	**Total points**	/25	**Total points**	/25

Show your project choices to your teacher by: _____

All of your projects are due on: _____

Differentiated Instruction for ESL Learners ©2013 Hubbert and Nieminen

Greetings, Responses, and Introductions
Dialogue List

Create Dialogues in English
according to target country customs using the following ideas:

- Greet and respond with 5 different people in the class. Include 3 lines per person in the dialogue.

- Greet and ask a store clerk for specific items.

- Call a restaurant, doctor, or dentist to make a reservation or appointment.

- Call your Grandma or other relative to ask her to come for dinner.

- Call your teacher or friend about homework that you missed when you were sick.

- You have a new friend with you when going to the movies with a group of friends. Introduce your new friend to everyone.

- Use pictures from a magazine to ask a classmate questions.

- Use pictures from a magazine to help you write a conversation.

- Greet a friend and ask "How are you?" as you meet him or her on the street or at school.

- Create a cartoon or comic strip with dialogue.

- Your friend is coming to dinner at your house for the first time. Introduce him or her to your parents. Include parents in the dialogue.

- After dinner at a friend's house, thank the parents and say goodbye.

- Thank a relative for the birthday present he or she gave you. Tell him or her how much you liked it.

Differentiated Instruction for ESL Learners ©2013 Hubbert and Nieminen

Greetings, Responses, and Introductions Assessment Rubric

Required Content for each dialogue:

- ❖ Correct Grammar
- ❖ Correct Sentence Structure
- ❖ Correct Pronunciation
- ❖ Correct English Vocabulary

Name: _____ Date: _____ Hour: _____

Required elements	Total Points Possible	Points Earned
Grammar	5 points	____ / 5
Sentence structure	5 points	____ / 5
Pronunciation	5 points	____ / 5
English vocabulary	5 points	____ / 5
Quality of Presentation	**Total Points Possible**	**Points Earned**
Good volume	5 points	____ / 5
Speak clearly	5 points	____ / 5
Memorize the dialogue	5 points	____ / 5
Give written copy of the dialogue for teacher to read or for assessment	5 points	____ / 5
TOTAL POINTS POSSIBLE	**40 points**	**TOTAL POINTS EARNED ____ / 40**

Differentiated Instruction for ESL Learners   ©2013 Hubbert and Nieminen

Colors and Clothing

Select "Three-in-a-Row" to complete the tic-tac-toe.

Create a Scrapbook	Model Your Outfit	Write a Song or a Rap
Make a scrapbook of clothing with different colors using target vocabulary.	Model an outfit you wear to school. As you model, describe your outfit to the class in English.	Write and perform a song or a rap using the clothing and color vocabulary. 
Create a Matching Game	Your Choice! 	Design a PowerPoint
Make and play a matching game for clothing and colors.		Make a PowerPoint of different clothing items in different colors.
Make Paper Dolls	Put on a Fashion Show	Write a Script
Make paper dolls with different outfits. Describe your dolls to the class using English. 	Put on a fashion show for the class to enjoy. You will need to ask friends to model five outfits.	Write a script in English for a video that you make of people wearing different colored clothing.

➢ **Challenge 1**: <u>Design and Sew</u> a new outfit. Design, sew, and model a new outfit for the season.
➢ **Challenge 2**: <u>Design a Magazine</u> in English for the latest trends in fashion.

Design and Sew		Design a Magazine	
* Must be your original design	___/ 5	* Name your magazine	___/ 5
* Draw the outfit in color	___/ 5	* Min. 10 fully covered pages with pictures	___/ 5
* Label clothing and colors on design in English	___/ 5	* Include short articles (can be cut from magazines)	___/ 5
* Give your outfit a name	___/ 5	* Include "advertisements"	___/ 5
* Sew and model your outfit	___/ 5	* Must be in color	___/ 5
Total points	___/ 25	**Total points**	___/ 25

Colors and Clothing Assessment Rubric

Create a Scrapbook		Model Your Outfit		Write a Song or a Rap	
* Min. 5.5 x 8.5 in., bound book	/5	* Include a min. of 6 items of clothing	/5	* 1-2 minutes long	/5
* Include a min. of 20 items of clothing	/5	* Use a min. of 5 colors	/5	* Include a min. of 15 vocabulary words	/5
* Illustrate cover; include title and student name	/5	* Write clothing names and colors for teacher to read	/5	* Must have a melody	/5
* Label all clothing items with name and color(s)	/5	* Use complete sentences when writing and speaking	/5	* Perform live or play recording to class	/5
* Must be in color	/5	* Model your outfit for the class	/5	* Give recording or written copy of words for teacher to look at before performing	/5
Total points	/ 25	Total points	/ 25	Total Points	/ 25

Create a Matching Game		_____ !		Design a PowerPoint	
* 3 x 5 in. index cards	/5		/5	* Include 10 colored slides	/5
* Include a min. of 20 cards for 10 matches	/5		/5	* Title slide must include student name	/5
* Use correct spelling and grammar in English	/5		/5	* Label clothing with colors using correct grammar in English	/5
* Use color	/5		/5	* Add music to your PowerPoint	/5
* Include container or bag for cards	/5		/5	* Present to the class	/5
Total points	/ 25	Total points	/ 25	Total points	/ 25

Make Paper Dolls		Put on a Fashion Show		Write a Script	
* Make 2 dolls with 3 outfits for each doll	/5	* Include 5 differently dressed friends in the show	/5	* Min. 1-2 minutes long	/5
* Draw or use magazine or internet pictures	/5	* Write down your outfit descriptions for teacher to read	/5	* Include a min. of 10 colors	/5
* Must be in color	/5	* Add music to the show	/5	* Video and sound are very good	/5
* Pronounce clearly and correctly	/5	* Announce show to class with clear pronunciation in English	/5	* Give recording or written copy for teacher to read before the performance	/5
* Describe your paper dolls in English to the class	/5	* You and your friends have practiced enough to put on a great show	/5	* Play video for the class	/5
Total points	/ 25	Total points	/ 25	Total points	/ 25

Show your project choices to your teacher by: _____

All of your projects are due on: _____

Differentiated Instruction for ESL Learners ©2013 Hubbert and Nieminen

Teacher Tips Page for Section C

Standards

Classroom Objects

4.1 – 2LS	3.1 – 2SW +Tech	1.3 – 2W
1.3 – 2LS		1.1 – 1W
1.3 – 2W	1.1 – 2LS	3.1 – 4W +Math

➢ Challenge: 3.1 – 2RW +ELA
➢ Challenge: 1.2 – 2RW +ELA

School Subjects, Schedule, and Teachers

1.1 – 1SW	1.3 - 1RW	1.3 – 1SW
1.3 – 1LS		1.1 – 1RW
4.2 – 1RW	3.1 – 1SW +Music	1.3 – 1W

➢ Challenge 1: 1.3 – 1W
➢ Challenge 2: 1.1 – 1LS

Family Nouns

1.3 – 1W	1.3 – 2W	2.1 – 1RW
1.3 – 2LS		1.3 – 1RW
3.1 – 1W +Art	1.3 – 5W	3.2 – 5W +S.S.

THE ARTS

- ❖ **Preview Material**
  - o For videotaped or recorded products, it is always wise to preview the video or recording prior to class presentation.
- ❖ **Classroom Objects**
  - o Ideas for "Your Choice": Create a horror story about a "classroom object gone crazy", e.g.: a stapler that won't let you stop stapling or a whiteboard that absorbs students and they become animated characters on the board.
- ❖ **School Subjects, Schedule, and Teachers**
  - o Ideas for "Your Choice": Write a story or create a storyboard or a comic about the ideal substitute teacher.
- ❖ **Family Nouns**
  - o Ideas for "Your Choice": Write a song or poem about your family members using target vocabulary; may be factual or fictional.

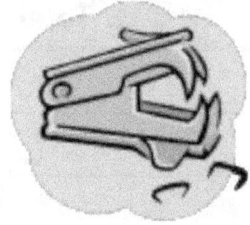 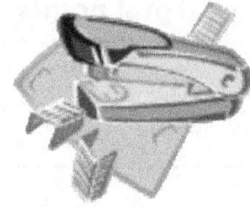

Classroom Objects

Select two projects to complete.

Create a Game	Make a PowerPoint	Draw a Floor Plan
Make a game with classroom objects using commands. Play the game with the class.	Design a PowerPoint with at least 20 classroom objects. 	Draw and label your classroom's floor plan in English. Include classroom objects.
Make a Video	**Your Choice!** 	**Create an Advertisement**
Create a video in English by having a friend record you while you are identifying classroom objects.		"Sell" your classroom! Create an advertisement to sell 10 classroom objects using target vocabulary.
Construct a Diorama	**Make Flashcards**	**Draw and Label a Graph**
Build the perfect 3-D classroom. What would you include?	Draw and label flashcards in English using at least 20 classroom objects. 	Count and graph a minimum of 10 different objects; e.g. 25 desks, 3 tables, 2 bookcases, etc.

- **Challenge 1:** <u>Illustrate a Children's Book</u> giving human qualities to the classroom objects.
- **Challenge 2:** <u>Create a Booklet</u> that has every possible classroom object. Every object must have one to three sentences that describe it.

Illustrate a Children's Book		Create a Booklet	
* Min. 5.5 x 8.5 in., bound book	___ / 5	* Min. 5.5 x 8.5 in., bound booklet	___ / 5
* Min. 10 pages, must be in color	___ / 5	* Min. 10 pages	___ / 5
* Label each object	___ / 5	* Illustrations must be in color	___ / 5
* Write sentence(s) for each picture	___ / 5	* Include title and author's name on illustrated front cover	___ / 5
* Include title and name of student on front cover, back cover with price, etc.	___ / 5	* Use correct spelling and grammar in sentences and labels	___ / 5
Total points	___ / 25	**Total points**	___ / 25

Classroom Objects Assessment Rubric

Create a Game		Make a PowerPoint		Draw a Floor Plan	
* Include 20 commands and objects in English	/5	* Include a min. of 10 content slides	/5	* Min. 8.5 x 11 in.	/5
* Write commands and objects on 3 x 5 in. cards	/5	* First slide must be the title slide with student name	/5	* Use graph paper	/5
* Game allows entire class to participate	/5	* Label each object in English	/5	* Label classroom objects in English	/5
* Write simple and complete rules	/5	* Must be in color	/5	* Must be in color	/5
* Give rules for the teacher to read before playing	/5	* Present to class	/5	* Present and/or display the drawing in the classroom	/5
Total points	/25	**Total points**	/25	**Total Points**	/25

Make a Video		_____!		Create an Advertisement	
* Include min. of 20 objects	/5		/5	* Min 8.5 x 11 in.	/5
* Turn in a written list of objects for teacher to read before presentation	/5		/5	* Include names of all items; use your imagination	/5
* Quality of video and sound is excellent	/5		/5	* Include a color picture of each item	/5
* Speak in a clear voice and use correct pronunciation	/5		/5	* Create a slogan	/5
* Present the video to the class	/5		/5	* Prices of all items must be in target country currency	/5
Total points	/25	**Total points**	/25	**Total points**	/25

Construct a Diorama		Make Flashcards		Draw and Label a Graph	
* Min. 1 shoebox size, max. 3 shoeboxes	/5	* Use 3 x 5 in. index cards	/5	* Give your graph a title and label the axes	/5
* Min. 20 objects, 5 must be 3-D objects	/5	* Include 20 objects in color	/5	* Make a list of all objects and include the number of objects	/5
* Label all objects in English	/5	* Draw picture of the object on one side; write the word or phrase on the other side	/5	* Graph must have correct spacing and format	/5
* Decorate all surfaces	/5	* Include container or bag for cards	/5	* You must use English	/5
* Name your diorama	/5	* Play the game with a classmate	/5	* Display graph in class	/5
Total points	/25	**Total points**	/25	**Total points**	/25

Show your project choices to your teacher by: _____

All of your projects are due on: _____

School Subjects, Schedule, and Teachers

Select "Three-in-a-Row" to complete the tic-tac-toe.

Write and Perform a Skit	Write a School Schedule	Survey Your Classmates
Write and perform a skit in English with another student. Ask about each other's schedule.	Make a schedule of subjects, times, and teachers' names for a new student. Use target vocabulary.	Ask your classmates what subjects they take. Share the results in a graph.
Interview Your Teachers — Interview your teachers to find out some interesting information about them. Share the information with your classmates.	**Your Choice!** 	**Tweet** — Pretend you are using *Twitter*. Use the 140 character limit to tweet about your daily schedule, teachers, or favorite subject. Use English.
Make a Poster — Research a typical school day schedule in your native country. Share the information on a poster in English.	**Write a Song or Rap** — Write an original song in English about your favorite subject(s).	**Make a 3-D Timeline** — Make a 3-D timeline of your school schedule with subjects and extra-curricular activities.

- **Challenge 1**: Draw a Floor Plan of your school with teachers' names, classroom numbers, subjects, and times for each of your classes. Include all other rooms in the school that you know.
- **Challenge 2**: Write a Questionnaire asking classmates about their favorite subjects. Graph the results and present them to the class in English.

Draw a Floor Plan		Write a Questionnaire	
* Min. 8.5 x 11 in. paper	___/ 5	* Write out questions and tally results	___/ 5
* Use graph paper	___/ 5	* Use 8.5 x 11 in. graph paper, graph must cover at least half of the paper	___/ 5
* Label all objects in English	___/ 5	* Title graph and label axes	___/ 5
* Must be in color	___/ 5	* Include your original tally sheet	___/ 5
* Make it as close to scale as possible	___/ 5	* Present to and display in class	___/ 5
Total points	___/ 25	**Total points**	___/ 25

School Subjects, Schedule, and Teachers Assessment Rubric

Write and Perform a Skit		Write a School Schedule		Survey Your Classmates	
* Min. 5 lines per speaker	____/5	* Max. 5.5 x 8.5 in. card	____/5	* 8.5 x 11 in., graph must cover at least half of paper	____/5
* Use vocabulary words correctly	____/5	* Use heavy paper, cardstock, or index card	____/5	* Title graph and label axes in English	____/5
* Script must be turned in for teacher to read	____/5	* Neatly written or typed	____/5	*Use color in the graph	____/5
* Include costumes and important items	____/5	* Title the schedule and number each class	____/5	* Include your original tally sheet	____/5
* Perform in front of the class	____/5	* Display in class	____/5	* Display in class	____/5
Total points	____/25	**Total points**	____/25	**Total Points**	____/25
Interview Your Teachers		_____!		Tweet	
* Ask each teacher 5 questions in English	____/5		____/5	* Write 1-2 Tweets	____/5
* Interview 2-4 teachers	____/5		____/5	* Use complete sentences	____/5
* Write questions and answers in English	____/5		____/5	* Tweets must be typed like *Twitter*	____/5
* Include teacher's name, family, pets, and hobbies	____/5		____/5	* Use 100-140 characters	____/5
* Share with the class	____/5		____/5	* Use target vocabulary	____/5
Total points	____/25	**Total points**	____/25	**Total points**	____/25
Make a Poster		Write a Song or a Rap		Make a 3-D Timeline	
* Standard poster size	____/5	* 1-2 minutes long	____/5	* No larger than 3 ft. long, 1 ft. high	____/5
* Illustrations in color (drawings, magazine or internet pictures)	____/5	* Include a min. of 6 different lines in English	____/5	* Include times of all subjects, classes, breaks, and lunch	____/5
* Name your poster	____/5	* Give written words for teacher to read	____/5	* Use color	____/5
* Include the schedule	____/5	* Must have a melody	____/5	* Give your timeline a title	____/5
* Share the poster and display it in class	____/5	* Perform live or play a recording of your song	____/5	* Glue or tape a 3-D object or picture next to each subject or time	____/5
Total points	____/25	**Total points**	____/25	**Total points**	____/25

Show your project choices to your teacher by: _____

All of your projects are due on: _____

Differentiated Instruction for ESL Learners ©2013 Hubbert and Nieminen

Family Nouns

Select "Three-in-a-Row" to complete the tic-tac-toe.

Create a Family Tree	Draw a Family Album	Write a Story
Illustrate and label the tree diagram with blood relatives in English. 	Pick ten of your family members, draw and label each in English. Describe each with a complete sentence in English using at least three adjectives.	Write a story about a family using the target vocabulary of family nouns. Story can be factual or fictional. 
Write a News Report	Your Choice!	Create a Children's Book
Write a news report about your family. Make it exciting! Report it to the class.		Illustrate and label a children's book in English about family members.
Paint a Mural	Map it Out	Make a Timeline
Paint a mural about your family. Illustrate and label at least six family members. 	Label a map with the locations of your family members' homes.	Label each family member's name and year of birth in chronological order in English. 

33

Differentiated Instruction for ESL Learners ©2013 Hubbert and Nieminen

Family Nouns Assessment Rubric

Create a Family Tree		Draw a Family Album		Write a Story	
* Min. 12 x 18 in. size	/5	* Min. 5.5 x 8.5 in. bound album	/5	* 1-3 paragraphs	/5
* Begin the tree with your grandparents	/5	* Include one family member per page	/5	* Neatly written or typed	/5
* Must include color	/5	* Draw each person in color	/5	* Use target vocabulary	/5
* Draw or use real photos of each person	/5	* Describe each person using 3 adjectives; use complete sentences	/5	* Include beginning, middle, and end of story	/5
* Label each person with the family relationship	/5	* Present to the class	/5	* Read your story to the class	/5
Total points	/ 25	Total points	/ 25	Total Points	/ 25

Write a News Report		_____ !		Create a Children's Book	
* Type it in English	/5		/5	* Min. 5.5 x 8.5 in. bound book	/5
* Answer who, what, when, where, why, and how	/5		/5	* Include all family nouns	/5
* Give a copy to the teacher before the performance	/5		/5	* Include illustrations in color for each page	/5
* Include photo or visual with comment (caption)	/5		/5	* Cover must have title and student name	/5
* Your performance is smooth; you practiced well	/5		/5	* Use correct spelling and grammar	/5
Total points	/ 25	Total points	/ 25	Total points	/ 25

Paint a Mural		Map it Out		Make a Timeline	
* Min. 1 standard poster size, max. size about 4 standard posters	/5	* Min. 8.5 X 11 in.	/5	* No larger than 3 ft. long, 1 ft. high	/5
* Background must represent your native country	/5	* Include a min. of 7 different locations	/5	* Divide the timeline into equal yearly units	/5
* Give your mural a title	/5	* Draw your map by hand or use a real map	/5	* Use color	/5
* Must be in color	/5	* Label locations with family noun(s) and name(s) in English	/5	* Include 5 important world events during the timeline years	/5
* Labels must include family noun in English (e.g. mother, father, sister, etc.)	/5	* Include map key and compass rose	/5	* Glue or tape an important object or illustration next to each birth date	/5
Total points	/ 25	Total points	/ 25	Total points	/ 25

Show your project choices to your teacher by: _____

All of your projects are due on: _____

Unit 2: Connecting with Culture

- ❖ Teacher Tips for Pages 35 to 42 36
- ❖ General Heritage and Customs 37
- ❖ Customs and Traditions 39
- ❖ Family Life 41
- ❖ Foods 43
- ❖ Teacher Tips for Pages 44 to 51 45
- ❖ Traditional Clothing 46
- ❖ Modern Clothing 48
- ❖ Arts and Education 50
- ❖ Famous People 52

Teacher Tips for Pages 35 to 42

Standards

General Heritage and Customs

4.2 – 1W	3.2 – 5LS	2.1 – 5W
2.1 – 5W	1.3 – 5W +Tech	3.1 – 5LS +Art
2.2 – 5LS +Tech	2.1 – 5W +Art	1.3 – 5W

Customs and Traditions

4.2 – 1SW	4.2 – 5S
2.1 – 5S	3.2 – 1SW
4.2 – 5W	3.2 – 5S
4.2 – 5W	4.2 – 5W

Family Life

4.2 – 5LS	2.1 – 5W	5.1 – 1SL
1.3 – 1W		1.3 – 1SW
1.3 – 1W	1.3 – 5LS	3.2 – 1W

Foods

2.2 – 5W	2.1 – 5S	2.2 – 5LS
3.2 – 5SW		3.2 – 5W
2.2 – 5W	2.2 – 5W	1.3 – 5W

➢ **Challenge 1**: 2.2 – 5W
➢ **Challenge 2**: 2.1 – 5W

❖ **Preview Material**
    o For videotaped or recorded products, it is always wise to preview the video or recording prior to class presentation.

Familiarize yourself with the Teacher's Choice Project format prior to handing out the *Customs and Traditions* sheet to students.

Teacher's Choice Projects:
    o Excellent group projects.
    o Teacher chooses groups.
    o Teacher assigns project(s) for each group.
    o Teacher gives groups a time limit on presentation.
    o Group presents its project together; all members must be part of presentation.
    o Projects make great displays for the classroom.
    o OPTIONAL: Have each group come up with 2-3 questions about their topic which the teacher then transfers onto a worksheet for students to complete as a quiz.
    o TECHNOLOGY IS FABULOUS: Teachers have students email the questions to them which the teachers then proofread, copy and paste to a document: quiz created. ☺
    o Below is the "**Student Version**" for you to copy or write on the board, if needed.

Teacher's Choice Projects:
    o Teacher chooses groups.
    o Teacher assigns project(s) for each group.
    o Groups have a time limit on presentation: min._____, max. _____ minutes.
    o Group presents project *together;* all members must be part of presentation.
    o Each group creates 2-3 questions about its topic and emails the questions to the teacher.

The General Heritage and Customs of _____.

Complete one from Column I and one more from Columns II or III.

Column I	Column II	Column III
Create a Menu and Write a Recipe Card Make a menu for at least five items and write a detailed recipe card for one dish.	**Describe Family Life in an English speaking country** Research the structure and culture of a typical family in a target country. Answer questions such as: Who makes the rules? Is it the parents or grandparents? Describe five facts in your speech.	**Write a News Report about the Facts and Figures** Write a news report about the facts and figures of an English speaking country. Include flag, currency, economy, geography, climate, and government.
Write about the Education, Language(s), and Religion(s) Write about the educational system, languages, and the religions practiced in an English speaking country. Use complete sentences.	**Create a PowerPoint of the Major Historical Events** Make a PowerPoint of the major historical events of an English speaking country.	**Create a PowerPoint on Visual and Performing Arts** Make a PowerPoint displaying important visual and performing arts or artists in an English speaking country.
Create a PowerPoint about Clothing Make a PowerPoint about the traditional and present-day clothing of an English speaking country.	**Draw a Mural of Jobs and Hobbies** Draw or paint a mural with at least 10 different jobs and hobbies of an English speaking country.	**Create a Collage of Customs and Traditions for Different Holidays** Make a collage of the customs and traditions for different holidays in an English speaking country.

Differentiated Instruction for ESL Learners ©2013 Hubbert and Nieminen

General Heritage and Customs Assessment Rubric

Column I	Column II	Column III
Create a Menu and Write a Recipe Card	**Describe Family Life**	**Write a News Report about the Facts and Figures**
* List a min. of 5 menu items ___/5	* Min. 5 characteristics ___/5	* Min. 2 minutes long ___/5
* Menu must be in color with illustrations ___/5	* Typed or neatly written ___/5	* Include a min. of 3 visual aids ___/5
* Neatly written or typed in English ___/5	* Turn in copies of original research material ___/5	* Include flag, currency, economy, geography, climate, and government ___/5
* Write a recipe card of an authentic ethnic dish ___/5	* Give typed or written copy for teacher to read before performance ___/5	* Give taped or written script for teacher to look at before performance ___/5
* Use correct spelling ___/5	* Present to class ___/5	* Play video or perform live ___/5
Total points ___/25	**Total points ___/25**	**Total Points ___/25**
Write about the Education, Languages, and Religions	**Create a PowerPoint of the Major Historical Events**	**Create a PowerPoint on Visual and Performing Arts**
* Min. 1-3 paragraphs ___/5	* Min. 8-10 content slides ___/5	* Min. 10 content slides in color ___/5
* Must be in English ___/5	* Min. 5-8 historical events ___/5	* Min. 10 different works or artists ___/5
* Must be typed; give a copy for teacher to read ___/5	* Include student name on the title slide ___/5	* Include student name on the title slide ___/5
* Use complete sentences and correct spelling ___/5	* Pictures or clip art in color, when possible ___/5	* Include information about the artist on each slide ___/5
* Present to class ___/5	* Present to class ___/5	* Present to class ___/5
Total points ___/25	**Total points ___/25**	**Total points ___/25**
Create a PowerPoint about Clothing	**Draw a Mural of Jobs and Hobbies**	**Create a Collage of Customs and Traditions for Different Holidays**
* Min. 10 content slides ___/5	* Min. 24 x 54 in. ___/5	* Standard poster size ___/5
* Include student name on the title slide ___/5	* Include a min. of 10 illustrations in color ___/5	* Use magazines or internet pictures in color ___/5
* Include pictures in color with 5 traditional and 5 modern outfits ___/5	* Draw neatly or use magazine or online pictures ___/5	* Include a min. of 5 major holidays ___/5
* Write a brief description of each clothing item or outfit ___/5	* Label each job or hobby (can be on the other side) ___/5	* Label pictures in English ___/5
* Present to class ___/5	* Display in the classroom ___/5	* Display in the classroom ___/5
Total points ___/25	**Total points ___/25**	**Total points ___/25**

Show your project choices to your teacher by: _____

All of your projects are due on: _____

Differentiated Instruction for ESL Learners   ©2013 Hubbert and Nieminen

Customs and Traditions ~ Teacher's Choice

Gestures for Communication
- Social
- Business
- **Create an Illustrated List** of gestures in an English speaking country

Holidays, Customs, and Traditions
- Compare the most important ones with your home country using a **Venn Diagram**
- Choose **One in Detail** and decide how to present it to the class

Introductions
- Friends
- Acquaintances
- Business associates
- **Write Dialogues**

Independence Day
- History
- Celebrations
- **Make a Timeline**

Religious Customs
- Births, deaths, weddings, divorces, etc.
- Christenings and baptisms
- Important religious events of a target country
- **Answer Questions** and decide how to present them to the class

School Customs, Dating Customs, and Sports Traditions
- School Customs: Compare your customs and an English speaking country's customs in a **Venn Diagram**
- Dating Customs: Compare your customs and an English speaking country's customs in a **Venn Diagram**
- Sports Traditions: **Make a Poster to Compare**

Customs and Traditions Assessment Rubric

Gestures for Communication~ Illustrated List	
* Use a min. of 5 gestures	____/5
* Illustrations in color	____/5
* Include social and business gestures	____/5
* Neatly written or computer generated	____/5
* Present to the class	____/5
Total points	____/25

Holidays, Customs, and Traditions Venn Diagram	
* Min. 8.5 x 11 in.	____/5
* Title the diagram and label each part	____/5
* Min. of 15 holidays, customs, and traditions	____/5
* Must be neatly drawn in color	____/5
* Present to the class	____/5
Total points	____/25

Holidays, Customs, and Traditions ~ One in Detail	
* Name of holiday/custom/tradition in English	____/5
* Illustrations and/or visual aids in color	____/5
* Include foods, decorations, and/or costumes	____/5
* Include answers to the questions of when, where, how, and why	____/5
* Present to the class	____/5
Total points	____/25

Introductions~ Dialogues	
* Create one dialogue for each introduction	____/5
* Include a min. of 4-6 lines for each dialogue	____/5
* Neatly written or typed	____/5
* Write a paragraph in English explaining introductions in an English speaking country	____/5
* Present to the class	____/5
Total points	____/25

Independence Day Timeline	
* No larger than 3 ft. x 1 ft.	____/5
* List 7-10 historical events that led to the independence day of the target country	____/5
* Describe each date or event	____/5
* Explain the independence day celebration in one paragraph on a separate sheet	____/5
* Attach an illustration or object in color next to each event or date on the timeline	____/5
Total points	____/25

Religious Customs ~ Answer Questions	
* What importance does religion have in the society of the target country?	____/5
* What are the major religion(s)?	____/5
* How important is religion in the births, deaths, weddings, etc. of the target country?	____/5
* What are the significant religious celebrations or events in the target country?	____/5
* Present to the class in a creative way	____/5
Total points	____/25

School or Dating Customs Venn Diagram	
* Min. 8.5 x 11 in. paper	____/5
* Title the diagram and label each part	____/5
* Compare a min. of 10 customs of your home country and a target country	____/5
* Must be neatly drawn	____/5
* Use color	____/5
Total points	____/25

Sports Traditions ~ Poster to Compare	
* Standard poster size	____/5
* Title the poster	____/5
* Write down each comparison on the poster	____/5
* Illustrations must be in color	____/5
* Label each tradition by country	____/5
Total points	____/25

Show your project choices to your teacher by: _____

All of your projects are due on: _____

Differentiated Instruction for ESL Learners ©2013 Hubbert and Nieminen

Family Life

Select "Three-in-a-Row" to complete the tic-tac-toe.

Make and Draw a Venn Diagram	Make a Storyboard	Blog about It
Compare families and traditions of a target country with your native country. Share your Venn diagram with the class verbally.	Create a storyboard about one family tradition in detail or several family traditions in general from a target country. 	Find a blog in English about family life and engage in conversation with a person about his or her everyday family life.
Make a Lost Pet Ad	Your Choice! 	Make a Photo Album
Create a lost pet ad for your pet. Choose a target country pet. Your ad can be imaginary.		Create a photo album about a teenage celebrity and his or her family and pets. Label each picture with names and describe each family member.
Write a Letter	Design a Pets Poster	Give a Speech: General and Nonverbal Family Rules and Traditions*
Pretend you are a person in the target country. Tell someone about traditions that you have in your family.	Draw and describe common pets in an English speaking country. 	Find out general and nonverbal family rules and traditions in a target country. Present your information to the class in a speech.

*For example, in Finland, there is a nonverbal rule that when you walk into someone's house, you remove your shoes.

Family Life Assessment Rubric

Make and Draw a Venn Diagram	Make a Storyboard	Blog about It
* Compare min. of 12 items ____/5	* Min. 12 x 18 in. ____/5	* Min. of 5 blog entries ____/5
* Draw neatly ____/5	* Min. of 6 story squares ____/5	* Use English ____/5
* Name the Venn and the sections of the Venn ____/5	* Each square must have an illustration and an explanation of the tradition ____/5	* Ask important and appropriate questions using complete sentences ____/5
* Color and decorate the Venn diagram ____/5	* Neatly written and drawn or computer generated ____/5	* Print out the conversations and turn them in to the teacher ____/5
* Share with the class ____/5	* Illustrations in color ____/5	* Share your blog entries with the class ____/5
Total points ____/25	**Total points** ____/25	**Total Points** ____/25

Make a Lost Pet Ad	_____!	Make a Photo Album
* Min. 8.5 x 11 in. ____/5	____/5	* Min. 5x 7 in., bound album ____/5
* Describe your pet and illustrate your pet in color ____/5	____/5	* Include a min. of 10 pages ____/5
* Use correct spelling and grammar ____/5	____/5	* Name each person ____/5
* Must have words "lost pet" in English ____/5	____/5	* Describe each person with a complete sentence ____/5
* Include contact information ____/5	____/5	* Present to the class ____/5
Total points ____/25	**Total points** ____/25	**Total points** ____/25

Write a Letter	Design a Pets Poster	Give a Speech: Family Rules and Traditions
* Min. 1-3 paragraphs ____/5	* Standard poster size ____/5	* Min. 2 minutes long ____/5
* Typed, double- spaced, max. size 14 pt. font ____/5	* Pick top 5-10 pets ____/5	* Include a min. of 2 visual aids ____/5
* Use correct spelling and grammar and use English language *letter format* ____/5	* Describe and label each pet in English ____/5	* Give outline to teacher 2 days before presentation ____/5
* Share typical activities in the lives of a target country family ____/5	* Give your poster a name ____/5	* Write speech on note cards (index cards) ____/5
* Read the letter to the class ____/5	* Illustrations in color (drawings, magazine or internet pictures) ____/5	* Your speech is smooth (you have practiced enough) ____/5
Total points ____/25	**Total points** ____/25	**Total points** ____/25

Show your project choices to your teacher by: _____

All of your projects are due on: _____

Foods

Select "Three-in-a-Row" to complete the tic-tac-toe.

Make a Recipe Book	Set the Table	Make a Dish
Create a recipe book for typical foods in an English speaking country. Use one category of foods or several different categories of foods.	Set a table for four in the custom of the target country. List and illustrate the table setting. Build a diorama or, if possible, use real items to display the table setting for your class.	Make a typical dish from an English speaking country. Include a recipe and share the dish with your class. 
Plan a Menu	Your Choice! 	Plan a Traditional Party
Plan a menu for one week for a typical family in an English speaking country. Choose how you will present your menu to the class.		Plan a traditional party with 6-10 items. Include drinks, appetizers, entrees, desserts, party ware, decorations, etc.
Make a Picture Album	Make a Collage	Make a Flipbook
Create a picture album with 20 food items from an English speaking country. Include pictures and labels for the food items. 	Make a collage of different menu items for an English speaking country.	Make a flipbook which includes recipes and illustrations.

- **Challenge 1:** Using target country staples and spices <u>Create an Original Dish</u> that you like. Make the dish, include the recipe, and share with the class.
- **Challenge 2:** <u>Write and Illustrate a Complete Menu</u> for a restaurant using target country dishes.

Create an Original Dish		**Write and Illustrate a Complete Menu**	
* Min. 5.5 x 8.5 in. recipe card	___ / 5	* Min. 8.5 x 11 in.	___ / 5
* Include photo or illustration of the dish	___ / 5	* Include a min. of 2 pages of menu items with descriptions	___ / 5
* Give a copy of recipe to teacher before the presentation	___ / 5	* Illustrate the front cover	___ / 5
* Make the dish	___ / 5	* Include prices	___ / 5
* Share the dish with class	___ / 5	* Neatly written and drawn or computer generated	___ / 5
Total points	___ / 25	**Total points**	___ / 25

Foods Assessment Rubric

Make a Recipe Book		Set the Table		Make a Dish	
* Min. 5.5 x 8.5 in., bound book	/5	* Make a diorama or provide the real setting	/5	* Min. 5.5 x 8.5 in. recipe card	/5
* Include a min. of 10 typical recipes	/5	* Make placemats	/5	* Include illustration of dish	/5
* Illustrate the cover and include the title and your name	/5	* Give blueprint of table setting for teacher to look at	/5	* Give recipe for teacher to see before presentation	/5
* Illustrate each recipe in color	/5	* Write 5 commands which tell someone to set the table	/5	* Share recipe with the class	/5
* Neatly written and drawn or computer generated	/5	* Present to class	/5	* Share the dish with the class	/5
Total points	/25	**Total points**	/25	**Total Points**	/25

Plan a Menu		_____!		Plan a Traditional Party	
* Plan a menu for 7 days with 3 meals per day	/5		/5	* Create the menu and the plan for the party	/5
* Include times of meals	/5		/5	* State the purpose of the party	/5
* Draw a picture of a dish for each day	/5		/5	* Describe each item in the plan	/5
* Neatly written and drawn or computer generated	/5		/5	* Illustrate each food item	/5
* Present to class	/5		/5	* Neatly written and drawn or computer generated	/5
Total points	/25	**Total points**	/25	**Total points**	/25

Make a Picture Album		Make a Collage		Make a Flipbook	
* Min. 5.5 x 8.5 in., bound album	/5	* Min. 12 x 18 in.	/5	* Min. 8.5 x 11 in., folded	/5
* 20 illustrations in color	/5	* Include a min. of 10 items	/5	* Include a min. of 5 recipes	/5
* Include a min. of 10 pages	/5	* Label each menu item in English (label can be on the reverse side)	/5	* Recipes are from an English speaking country (include sources of recipes)	/5
* Label each food item	/5	* Give your collage a title	/5	* Give your flipbook a title	/5
* Write the title on the front cover and your name on the back cover	/5	* Illustrations in color (drawings, magazine or internet pictures)	/5	* Illustrations in color (can be magazine or internet photos)	/5
Total points	/25	**Total points**	/25	**Total points**	/25

Show your project choices to your teacher by: _____

All of your projects are due on: _____

Teacher Tips for Pages 46 to 53

Standards

Traditional Clothing		Modern Clothing		
2.1 – 5LS	2.1 – 5RW	2.1 – 1SW	1.3 – 1SW	1.3 – 1SW
2.1 – 5W	2.1 – 5W +Tech	➢ Challenge: 1.3 – 1SW		
2.1 – 5W +Art	2.1 – 5W			

Arts and Education			Famous People		
2.2 – 2W +Art	1.3 – 1,5	1.3 – 5W	3.2 – 1W	1.3 – 1W	1.3 – 1W
3.1 – 2W		3.1 – 2SW	1.3 – 1RW	1.3 – 1W	1.2 – 1LS
1.3 – 5W	1.3 – 1W	1.2 – 1W	1.3 – 1LS	3.2 – 1SW	

➢ Challenge: 1.3/Art- 5W

❖ **Preview Material**
  o For videotaped or recorded products, it is always wise to preview the video or recording prior to class presentation.

❖ **Traditional Clothing**
  o Examples for English speaking countries: Australia: Aborigines, New Zealand: Maoris, Canada: Provincial costumes, England: e.g. Scotland, USA: Native Americans.

❖ **Modern Clothing**
  o Prior to projects, have students bring old magazines, clothing catalogues, newspaper ads, and internet pictures portraying target country fashions. The projects are enhanced by visiting the computer lab so that students can see authentic and current fashions online.

❖ **Arts and Education:** Example of an Education Recipe Card:

Recipe for Finland's Educational System	
1 cup of excellent teacher salaries	A heaping helping of no organized school sports
5 tbsp. of quality teachers	4 barrels of quality, hot food every school day
15 tsp. of recess every hour	2 cups of the same books, same lesson strategies and timelines throughout the country

Use these ingredients as follows:
1. Entrance to university and teacher training is based on talent, not on whether you have the money for college. Schooling is free, but exams for admittance are vigorous.
2. Studies have shown that taking a long enough break often enough improves one's ability to learn and retain information. In Finland, students go outside, rain or shine, for 15 minutes every hour.
3. Sports and recreation are separate from the school environment. No money or time is spent from the school budget on organized sports.
4. School books, supplies, and quality, warm food are all provided to everyone free of charge.
5. Quality food is served: homemade-style casseroles, soup, salads, etc. No hamburgers, hot dogs, or fast food-type fare is served.
6. When/if you have to move during a school year, you will fit right in.

❖ **Famous People**
  o Ideas for "Your Choice": Make a collage of famous people, and then cut it into puzzle pieces for friends to put together. Follow a famous person on Twitter or Facebook for a week, and then write a summary about his/her activities. Write an obituary for a living celebrity.

 # Traditional Clothing and Costumes

To complete this project, you will need to choose two assignments.

1. Choose a speech *or* an essay.
2. Choose a visual presentation of the traditional clothing and costumes.
   - Examples of traditional clothing and costumes for English speaking countries: Australia: Aborigines, New Zealand: Maoris, Canada: Provincial costumes, England: Scotts, USA: Native Americans.
3. Show your project choices to your teacher by: _____.
4. All of your projects are due on: _____.

Each province/state/area in the target country has a different costume. Select a speech to give *or* an essay to write. Your task is to answer the following questions:

- ❖ Why do the countries have different costumes?
- ❖ When are they worn?
- ❖ What do the colors signify?
- ❖ Who wears the costumes?
- ❖ What do the costumes symbolize?
- ❖ Where are the costumes worn? (E.g. For what occasion(s) are they worn?)

After choosing a speech or an essay, pick *one* of the four choices below. This is for your visual presentation of the traditional clothing and costumes:

- ❖ <u>Create a Photo-folio.</u> Create a photo-folio of all the target country's traditional clothing. Include names of costumes and locations.
- ❖ <u>Make a PowerPoint.</u> Pick an area of an English speaking country (e.g. north, south, west, or east) and create a PowerPoint of the traditional costumes.
- ❖ <u>Make Paper Dolls.</u> Provide a detailed description of one type of costume from the target country. Include the man's and woman's costumes.
- ❖ <u>Design a Poster.</u> Pick an area of the country (e.g. north, south, west, or east) and provide a detailed description of five costumes in that area. Include the men's and women's costumes; draw and label each costume.

Traditional Clothing and Costumes Assessment Rubric

Choose one:

Give a Speech	
* Min. 2 minutes long	___/5
* Answer all questions clearly	___/5
* Give copy of speech for teacher to read before presentation	___/5
* Use notecards to read from during presentation	___/5
* Use good volume and clear pronunciation	___/5
Total points	___/25

Write an Essay	
* Min. 250 words	___/5
* Answer all questions clearly	___/5
* Type your essay in correct format	___/5
* Include where you found the information	___/5
* Use correct spelling and grammar	___/5
Total Points	___/25

Choose one:

Create a Photo-folio	
* Min. 5.5 x 8.5 in., bound book	___/5
* Include a min. of 10 costumes	___/5
* Label all costumes	___/5
* Must be in color	___/5
* Include title and student name on the cover page	___/5
Total points	___/25

Make a PowerPoint	
* Min. 10 slides of traditional costumes	___/5
* Include photo(s) and label(s) on each slide	___/5
* Must be in color	___/5
* Use correct spelling	___/5
* Title slide must include name of country and student name	___/5
Total points	___/25

Make Paper Dolls	
* Min. 1 detailed costume per gender	___/5
* Use heavy paper or poster board	___/5
* Must be in color	___/5
* Make a display stand for the paper dolls	___/5
* Label name of the costume and the target country on the display stand	___/5
Total points	___/25

Design a Poster	
* Standard poster size	___/5
* Include a min. of 5 costumes	___/5
* Give your poster a title	___/5
* Must be in color	___/5
* Label costumes with locations in the area	___/5
Total points	___/25

Modern Clothing

Students use clothing vocabulary in real life situations. For this project, students should research the target country's clothing customs. Through this project, students will realize that clothing is an important form of expression in all cultures.

1-3 person group	1-3 person group	1-3 person group
Create a Dialogue in English with a clothing store clerk or a friend talking about clothing items at a specific store. Write out the dialogue and include a description of the location of the store.	Describe your School's Dress Code in English. You may come up with a "new" dress code if you wish. You will need to present your rules to the "school board" or "the principal"; i.e. your teacher and class.	Create a Mini Catalog of modern fashions using English. The prices must be in a target country's currency. Present to class. You will need to describe the clothing. Give details of the fashion items that you include in the catalog.

All clothing choices must be school appropriate.

➢ **Challenge**: Be the Designer and put on a fashion show.

Be the Designer	
* Write a description for each outfit	____/5
* Write a brief bio of you, the designer	____/5
* Use correct grammar and spelling	____/5
* Include music during the show	____/5
* Ask five friends to model one outfit each and present to the class	____/5
Total points	____/ 25

Modern Clothing Assessment Rubric

⚡		☾		★	
* Include a min. of 3 clothing items	___/5	* Include a min. of 10 rules	___/5	* Min. 5.5 x 8.5 in. catalog	___/5
* Write a min. of 8-10 lines of dialogue	___/5	* Make a poster with the rules	___/5	* Include a min. of 15 items with prices	___/5
* Min. 1 visual aid or prop for each clothing item	___/5	* Neatly write or type information with correct grammar and spelling	___/5	* Describe each clothing item using correct grammar and spelling	___/5
* Neatly written or typed dialogue with correct grammar and spelling	___/5	* Each "rule" must have a picture as an example	___/5	* Illustrate each item in color (drawings, magazine or internet pictures)	___/5
* Each member of the group must present to the class	___/5	* Each member of the group must present to the class	___/5	* Each member of the group must present to the class	___/5
Total points	___/25	**Total points**	___/25	**Total Points**	___/25

Show your project choices to your teacher by: _____

All of your projects are due on: _____

49

Differentiated Instruction for ESL Learners ©2013 Hubbert and Nieminen

Arts and Education

Select "Three-in-a-Row" to complete the tic-tac-toe.

Draw a Portrait of an Artist	Build a Diorama	Write a Recipe Card
Research a famous visual artist. Write a paragraph about the artist and his work. Draw a portrait of the artist.	Take an online tour of a museum in an English speaking country. Build a diorama of the museum with historical and/or modern works of art.*	Write a "recipe card" for the educational system of an English speaking country. 
Design Book Covers or a Poster Make book covers or a poster of important literary works of an English speaking country.	**Your Choice!** 	**Perform Live on Stage** Research a composer or a performer. Write a speech about the person or give a performance of a work he or she has done.
Make a Brochure Create a brochure about different types of schools in an English speaking country.	**Write a Biography** Write a short bio and a description of the work of a choreographer or performance artist from an English speaking country.	**Write a Letter** Write a letter to an artist or an educator asking about his or her profession. 

*Other suggestions for the diorama: musical instruments, painting, sculpture, handiworks, cultural museum.

> **Challenge:** <u>Reproduce Art or a Building</u>. Reproduce an important piece of art from an English speaking country or an important building in the target country. If the original art is 3-D, you must reproduce it in 3-D, if 2-D, then 2-D, etc. A building may be drawn.

Reproduce Art or a Building	
* Min. 8.5 x 11 in. for 2-D, min. 5 in. height for 3-D	____/5
* Include a picture of the original art or building	____/5
* Reproduce with original color(s)	____/5
* Include bio of artist or architect	____/5
* Reproduction is of excellent quality	____/5
Total points	____/25

Arts and Education Assessment Rubric

Draw a Portrait of an Artist	Build a Diorama	Write a Recipe Card
* Min. 8.5 x 11 in. portrait size ___/5	* Approx. 10 x 32 x 28 in. or two standard shoe boxes ___/5	* Min. 5.5 x 8.5 in. recipe card ___/5
* Separate sheet for bio and work information of artist ___/5	* Include a min. of 10 art pieces ___/5	* Include a min. of 5 "ingredients" ___/5
* Info neatly written or typed ___/5	* Must be in color ___/5	* Illustration in color ___/5
* Draw the portrait using any style you want ___/5	* Decorate all surfaces ___/5	* Neatly written or typed with correct grammar and spelling ___/5
* Present to class ___/5	* Name of the museum and country must be on the title card ___/5	* Number the steps to complete the education recipe ___/5
Total points ___/25	Total points ___/25	Total Points ___/25

Design Book Covers or a Poster	_____!	Perform Live on Stage
* Book covers 8.5 x 11 in., standard size poster ___/5	___/5	* 1-2 minutes long ___/5
* Use a min. of 3 literary works ___/5	___/5	* Type the bio of composer or performer ___/5
* Title of work and author must be included for each work ___/5	___/5	* Written or typed outline of speech or performance for teacher to see before presentation ___/5
* Include a brief description of each work ___/5	* ___/5	* Your performance is smooth (practice is evident) ___/5
* Must be in color ___/5	___/5	* Present to the class ___/5
Total points ___/25	Total points ___/25	Total points ___/25

Make a Brochure	Write a Biography	Write a Letter
* 8.5 x 11 in., folded ___/5	* Neatly written or typed ___/5	* Must be typed in correct letter form ___/5
* Neatly written and drawn or computer generated ___/5	* Include name of the artist in the title ___/5	* Ask a min. of 5 questions ___/5
* Include a min. of 3 types of schools ___/5	* Use correct spelling, correct grammar, and complete sentences ___/5	* Write a min. of 1-3 paragraphs in English ___/5
* Illustrations in color ___/5	* Bio must have a min. of 5 facts about the artist ___/5	* Use correct grammar and spelling ___/5
* Title on the front cover, your name on back cover ___/5	* Include source(s); where you found the information ___/5	* Give a copy of letter and addressed envelope to teacher before mailing ___/5
Total points ___/25	Total points ___/25	Total points ___/25

Show your project choices to your teacher by: _____

All of your projects are due on: _____

Differentiated Instruction for ESL Learners ©2013 Hubbert and Nieminen

Famous people

Select one to complete.

Draw and Color a Picture
Draw and color a picture of a famous person in an English speaking country.

Who is it? Poster
Create a poster of a famous person. Include name, date of birth and/or death, what he or she is famous for, etc. Be creative.

Make a 3-D Timeline
Make a 3-D timeline of a famous person's life.

Make a Scrapbook
Design a scrapbook of a living famous person's life. Include copies of photos of the person.

Create a Collage
Make a collage about a famous person. Include important events in the person's life.

"Interview" a Famous Person
"Interview" your famous person of choice. Write the questions and include the answers. Get a classmate to ask the questions while you play the famous person.

You Be the Person
Act out a dialogue or monologue of the famous person you have chosen to be. Include important events in the life of the person.

Create a PowerPoint
Create an interactive PowerPoint for the class about a famous person from an English speaking country.

Your Choice!

Famous People Assessment Rubric

Draw and Color a Picture		Who is it? Poster		Make a 3-D Timeline	
* Min. 8.5 x 11 in.	/5	* Standard poster size	/5	* No larger than 3 ft. long, 1 ft. high in color	/5
* Write the sentences neatly and draw in color	/5	* Illustration(s) in color	/5	* Include a min. of 15 events	/5
* Brief bio of person and min. one sentence physical description of the person	/5	* Title must include the name of the famous person	/5	* Describe each event and include the date of the event	/5
* Include the reason why the person is famous	/5	* Write neatly or type information using correct grammar and spelling	/5	* Use correct grammar and spelling	/5
* Present to class or display in class	/5	* All information must be in English	/5	* Attach important object or illustration in 3-D form next to each event	/5
Total points	/ 25	**Total points**	/ 25	**Total Points**	/ 25

Make a Scrapbook		Create a Collage		"Interview" a Famous Person	
* Min. 5 x7 in., bound book	/5	* Standard poster size	/5	* 10 questions and answers neatly written or typed	/5
* Include a min. of 10 pages	/5	* Include a min. of 25 pictures	/5	* Q & A for teacher to read before presentation	/5
* Neatly write or type a sentence for each page	/5	* Label pictures (can be on the reverse side)	/5	* Include a prop, costume, or visual for the interview	/5
* Illustrations in color	/5	* Give your collage a title	/5	* Must be in English with correct grammar & spelling	/5
* Title on the front cover, name on the back cover	/5	* Make your collage colorful	/5	* Present to the class	/5
Total points	/ 25	**Total points**	/ 25	**Total points**	/ 25

You Be The Person		Create a PowerPoint		_____!	
* Min. 10-15 lines	/5	* Min. 8 content slides	/5		/5
* Give typewritten script for teacher to read	/5	* Title slide must include name of famous person	/5		/5
* Include important events in the famous person's life	/5	* Graphics in color	/5		/5
* Include prop or costume for the presentation	/5	* Use correct grammar and spelling	/5		/5
* Present to the class	/5	* Deliver the PowerPoint as an interactive presentation	/5		/5
Total points	/ 25	**Total points**	/ 25	**Total points**	/ 25

Show your project choices to your teacher by: _____

All of your projects are due on: _____

Unit 3: Home and Abroad

- ❖ Teacher Tips Page for Unit 3 55
- ❖ House and Home 56
- ❖ Neighborhood and Directions 55
- ❖ City and Transportation 60

Teacher Tips Page for Unit 3

Standards

House and Home

1.1 – 2W	3.2 – 1W +Art	1.3 – 2RW
2.2 – 2W		3.1 – 2W +Art
1.3 – 2SW	3.2 – 1W	1.3 – 2LSW

House and Home
Conversations with Family

All dialogues		
1.1 – 2LRW	1.2	1.3

Neighborhood and Directions

4.1 – 5W	1.3 – 1LSW	1.3 – 1LSW
1.3 – 1W		1.3 – 5W
1.3 – 5LS +Math	3.1 – 5W +S.S.	1.1 – 1LSW

City and Transportation

2.2 – 1, 5	1.3 – 5W	4.2 – 5W
1.3 – 2W		4.2 – 5LS +Tech
1.3 – 5W	4.1 – 5LS	1.3 – 5W

❖ **Preview Material**
  o For videotaped or recorded products, it is always wise to preview the video or recording prior to class presentation.

❖ **House and Home**
  o Use rubric on page 25 to assess dialogues, if needed.

❖ **Neighborhood and Directions:** Amazing Race Scavenger Hunt
  o This activity can be a group activity; the students make up the directions and create the "treasure" to be found. It can also be played in an "orienteering" fashion; the students get a stamp on their "passports" as they find the correct location through the directions given.

❖ **City and Transportation**
  ➢ **Challenge:** Create a Map Game of the capital city, a target country, or a section/region of a target country. Include destination places for tourists to visit and directions on how to get to the destinations. **Challenge**: 3.1/S.S. – **5W**

Create a Map Game	
* Min. 12 x 18 in. in size	___/5
* Include a min. of 5 destinations	___/5
* Include vocabulary expressions for directions on game activity cards	___/5
* Must be in English	___/5
* State the importance of the destination on game board spaces	___/5
Total points	___/25

House and Home

Select two projects to complete.

Describe Your Room	Be an Architect	Make a Matching Activity Worksheet
Describe your room in detail using target vocabulary.	Draw a typical house in an English speaking country. 	Create a matching activity using appliances and tableware vocabulary.
Make a List	Your Choice!	Build a Diorama
Create a list of objects using the category: *Outdoor Items and Objects*. (E.g. garage, mower, fence, garden, trees, etc.)		Build a diorama of your "dream room" using target vocabulary.
Draw a Floor Plan	Write a Journal	Describe and Draw
Draw a floor plan of your bedroom or another room in your house and label it using target vocabulary.	Write about daily chores you might need to do while living with a target country family. 	Describe furniture in your "dream house." Then have someone else draw it as you describe it aloud. This is a partner activity; both students must complete all requirements.

Students create a dialogue or have a conversation about the following topics:

- ❖ May I borrow the car?
- ❖ May I have money for new shoes or jeans, movie or a phone?
- ❖ What do you want for your birthday, Christmas, or graduation?
- ❖ What do you talk about at the dinner table?
- ❖ Ask a grandparent about his or her childhood, job, or favorite things.

Required Content for each dialogue:

- ❖ Correct Grammar
- ❖ Correct Sentence Structure
- ❖ Correct Pronunciation
- ❖ Correct Vocabulary Used

House and Home Assessment Rubric

Describe Your Room		Be an Architect		Make a Matching Activity Worksheet	
* Min. 10 items in the room	/5	* Min. 8.5 x 11 in.	/5	* Min. 8.5 x 11 in.	/5
* Neatly written or typed with correct grammar	/5	* Include surroundings (e.g. trees, flowers, roads, etc.)	/5	* Include a min. of 10 items	/5
* Use complete sentences	/5	* Must be in color	/5	* Use English	/5
* Use 2-3 adjectives to describe each item	/5	* Label 5 details in English	/5	* Draw illustrations on the left side in color	/5
* Draw a picture of the room in color	/5	* Use correct grammar; describe your house with 2-5 sentences in English	/5	* Write matching item names in random order on the right side	/5
Total points	/ 25	Total points	/ 25	Total Points	/ 25

Make a List		_____!		Build a Diorama	
* 8.5 x 11 in.	/5		/5	* Min. 1 shoebox size (or approx. 5x14x16 in.)	/5
* Include a min. of 20 items	/5		/5	* Label a min. of 10 items in English	/5
* Neatly written and drawn or computer generated	/5		/5	* Use a min. of three 3-D objects	/5
* Illustrate a min. of 10 items	/5		/5	* Decorate all surfaces	/5
* Title your list	/5		/5	* Title your diorama	/5
Total points	/ 25	Total points	/ 25	Total points	/ 25

Draw a Floor Plan		Write a Journal		Describe and Draw	
* Min. 12 x 18 in.	/5	* Include 10 chores	/5	* Describe 5 items in English	/5
* Min. 15 items (remember doors and windows)	/5	* Neatly written or typed with correct grammar & spelling	/5	* Type descriptions of the furniture	/5
* Draw the objects or use magazine or online pictures	/5	* Each entry must have dates and days of week	/5	* Use a min. of 5 descriptive terms (color, shape, size, etc. for each item)	/5
* Must be in color	/5	* Record at least one chore per day	/5	* Drawing must be in color	/5
* Present to the class and display in the classroom	/5	* Write in 1st person and in English	/5	* Turn in drawing; must be signed by student artist	/5
Total points	/ 25	Total points	/ 25	Total points	/ 25

Show your project choices to your teacher by: _____

All of your projects are due on: _____

Neighborhood and Directions

Select "Three-in-a-Row" to complete the tic-tac-toe.

Draw a Map	Make a List and Draw	Amazing Race Scavenger Hunt
Draw a map of your neighborhood. Label 12 destinations and/or streets on the map. 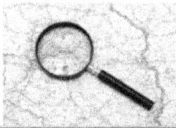	Draw a floor plan of the inside of your school. Make a list of directions that take the reader around the school.	Record audio or write instructions for classmates to find small treasures! This is a great partner activity. 
Make a Game Make a game using *directions* vocabulary to find destinations on the game board. Include rules on "how to play."	**Your Choice!**  	**Draw and Label a Map** Draw and label a map from your house to the school or another destination. Include directions to and from. Use English.
Survey and Graph Survey your classmates: How far do they live from the school or from your house? Map and graph the results. 	**Copy a Neighborhood Map** Pick a neighborhood (or choose the city center) in an English speaking country. Copy the map and label it with a minimum of 12 streets and locations, buildings, or businesses.	**Play "Blind Man's Bluff"** Give detailed instructions to classmates so they can find their way around the classroom while blindfolded. 

Differentiated Instruction for ESL Learners ©2013 Hubbert and Nieminen

Neighborhood and Directions Assessment Rubric

Draw a Map		Make a List and Draw		Amazing Race Scavenger Hunt	
* 8.5 x 11 in.	___/5	* 8.5 x 11 in.	___/5	* Include a min. of 10 instructions	___/5
* Write labels and streets in English	___/5	* Include 8 directions in English	___/5	* Clearly written and/or spoken directions in English	___/5
* Must be in color	___/5	* Use color in the floor plan	___/5	* Make or have a creative prize for each location that the players will visit	___/5
* Include compass rose and map key	___/5	* Label each room (e.g. office, gym, etc.) in English	___/5	* Create a "treasure bag" for each player	___/5
* Include a scale for the map (e.g. 1 in. = 1 mile)	___/5	* Present to class	___/5	* Lead the game	___/5
Total points	___/25	**Total points**	___/25	**Total Points**	___/25

Make a Game		_____!		Draw and Label a Map	
* Min. 11 x 17 in.	___/5		___/5	* 12 x 18 in. map	___/5
* Min. of 15 directions or instruction cards in English	___/5		___/5	* Label destination and departure point	___/5
* Include 4 game pieces and a creative title for the game	___/5		___/5	* Label 5 other locations on the way to the destination	___/5
* Must be in color	___/5		___/5	* Directions to and from in English	___/5
* Write a set of rules and directions	___/5		___/5	* Include a scale for the map (e.g. 1 in. = 1 mile)	___/5
Total points	___/25	**Total points**	___/25	**Total points**	___/25

Survey and Graph		Copy a Neighborhood Map		Play Blind Man's Bluff	
* Map and graph on separate sheets	___/5	* 12 x 18 in. map	___/5	* Write instructions on 3 x 5 in. index cards	___/5
* 8.5 x 11 in. each sheet	___/5	* Label 12 locations in English	___/5	* Use a min. of 5 different destinations	___/5
* Survey a min. of 10 classmates in English	___/5	* City must be in an English speaking country	___/5	* Include a min. of 10 directions in English	___/5
* Use color in the graph	___/5	* Must be in color	___/5	* Speak instructions clearly	___/5
* Label the map with classmate names	___/5	* Include compass rose and map key	___/5	* Lead the game	___/5
Total points	___/25	**Total points**	___/25	**Total points**	___/25

Show your project choices to your teacher by: _____

All of your projects are due on: _____

City and Transportation

Select "Three-in-a-Row" to complete the tic-tac-toe.

Draw a Cityscape	Make a Travel Brochure	Make a Venn Diagram
Draw a cityscape of a city in an English speaking country. 	Create a travel brochure for the capital city of one of the target countries. Include five tourist destinations in the city. Use English.	Compare city transportation in your city/town and a city/town of equal size in an English speaking country.
Write Instructions	Your Choice!	Make a PowerPoint
Write instructions on how to get around the capital city in an English speaking country. Pick a destination to go to from the airport, central bus, or train station.		Pick ten tourist destinations in an English speaking country. Make a PowerPoint presentation and be ready to share with the class.
Draw Postcards	Be a Travel Guide	Illustrate a Poster
Make three postcards to send to your family from a city or cities in the target country.	Pretend you are a travel guide on a bus trip. Videotape yourself telling all the tourists what they are looking at as you travel through a city in the target country.	Illustrate a poster sharing the major forms of transportation in one of the target countries. 

City and Transportation Assessment Rubric

Draw a Cityscape		Make a Travel Brochure		Make a Venn Diagram	
* 12 x 18 in.	___/5	* 8.5 x 11 in., folded	___/5	* 8.5 x 11 in.	___/5
* Use entire surface of the paper for the drawing	___/5	* Neatly written and drawn or computer generated	___/5	* Title the Venn diagram and label sections of the Venn	___/5
* Background outline must be hand drawn	___/5	* Include 5 destinations	___/5	* Include a min. of 15 items	___/5
* Foreground may use magazine cut-outs and must be in color	___/5	* Title fold must have a picture from the capital city	___/5	* Must be in color	___/5
* Title must include city and country names	___/5	* Must be in color	___/5	* Draw neatly	___/5
Total points	___/25	**Total points**	___/25	**Total Points**	___/25

Write Instructions		_____!		Make a PowerPoint	
* 8.5 x 11 in.	___/5		___/5	* Min. of 10 content slides	___/5
* Neatly written or typed instructions in English	___/5		___/5	* Include your name on the title slide	___/5
* Draw a map that contains the main roads of the capital city	___/5		___/5	* Include photo(s) and label(s) on each slide	___/5
* Map must be in color	___/5		___/5	* Must use color	___/5
* Label departure point and destination clearly	___/5		___/5	* Pronounce clearly and use good volume during presentation	___/5
Total points	___/25	**Total points**	___/25	**Total points**	___/25

Draw a Postcards		Be a Travel Guide		Illustrate a Poster	
* Use 4 x 6 in. poster board or heavy paper	___/5	* Must be 2-3 minutes long with correct pronunciation	___/5	* Standard poster size	___/5
* Picture on postcard must be an important location in the target country	___/5	* Create appropriate props or background for the "tour"	___/5	* Label each form of transportation in English	___/5
* Write message in English using correct grammar and spelling	___/5	* Give written monologue in English for teacher to read	___/5	* Illustrations in color (drawings, magazine or internet pictures)	___/5
* Label and color the picture	___/5	* Include min. of 8 city sights	___/5	* Title the poster	___/5
* Address the card and draw a postage stamp	___/5	* Present video to the class	___/5	* Include facts about each form of transportation	___/5
Total points	___/25	**Total points**	___/25	**Total points**	___/25

Show your project choices to your teacher by: _____

All of your projects are due on: _____

Unit 4: Body and Mind

- ❖ Teacher Tips Page for Unit 4 63
- ❖ Parts of the Body... 64
- ❖ Sports and Hobbies 66
- ❖ Feelings and Emotions 68
- ❖ Technology 70

Teacher Tips Page for Unit 4

Standards

Parts of the Body

1.3 – 2W	1.3 – 2W
3.1 – 1W +Art	1.2 – 2LSW
1.3 – 2W	1.3 – 2W

Sports and Hobbies

1.3 – 2LSW	3.1 - 3LS +Math	1.3 – 2W
1.2 – 2W		1.3 – 2SW
1.3 – 2W	1.3 – 2LSW	3.2 – 2W

➢ **Challenge 1**: 3.2 - 2R +Tech
➢ **Challenge 2**: 3.2 - 2R +Music

Feelings and Emotions

1.1 - 2W	1.1 – 2W
1.1 – 2W	4.1 – 2W
1.1 – 2W	1.1 – 2W
1.3 – 2LS	1.1 – 2W
3.1 – 2W +ELA	1.1 – 2W

Technology

5.1 – 2W	3.1 – 3LSW +Tech
3.1 – 2W +Tech	1.3 – 5W
2.2 – 5RW	2.2 – 5W
1.3 – 2W	1.3 – 2W

❖ **Preview Material**
  o For videotaped or recorded products, it is always wise to preview the video or recording prior to class presentation.

❖ **Parts of the Body**
  Examples of goofy remedies:
  o Tennis elbow~ Apply cornbread mixture and bake 30 minutes @ 250F.
  o Sore throat~ Hang upside down from the rafters for 15 minutes twice daily.
  o Stomach ache~ Perform 3 somersaults immediately after a meal of chili dogs.

❖ **Feelings and Emotions**
  o For "Use Vocabulary in a Sentence," have students illustrate each of the sentences for extra credit.

❖ **Sports and Hobbies**
  o Ideas for Your Choice: Be a Sports Announcer. Create a monologue with a minimum of 10 sentences using target vocabulary.

❖ **Technology**
  o Make a copy of the Facebook template on page 112-113 to show students and to familiarize yourself with the format.

Parts of the Body

Choose one project to complete.

Make a poster

Make a poster with labeled pictures of the parts-of-the-body vocabulary.

Draw a Self-Portrait

Draw a self-portrait and label parts of the body using target vocabulary.

Create a 3-D Mr. or Mrs. Potato Head

Create a 3-D Mr. or Mrs. Potato Head using a potato or clay, and other household or craft items.

Perform a Skit

You are the doctor: patients complain about different parts of the body. Make up silly remedies or cures for your patients.

Cut Out Photos of Celebrities

Cut out photos of celebrities from magazines; label the parts of their bodies.

Create a New Person

Cut out 12 different parts of the body from magazines to create a new person!

Differentiated Instruction for ESL Learners ©2013 Hubbert and Nieminen

Parts of the Body Assessment Rubric

Make a Poster	
* Standard poster size	___/5
* Include all target vocabulary	___/5
* Illustrations in color	___/5
* Label each illustration clearly	___/5
* Give your poster a title	___/5
Total points	___/25

Draw a Self-Portrait	
* Min. 8.5 x 11 in	___/5
* Label all parts of the body using target vocabulary	___/5
* Draw in color	___/5
* Give your drawing a title	___/5
* Display in class or share with class	___/5
Total points	___/25

Create a 3-D Mr. or Mrs. Potato Head	
* Min. 5 in. high	___/5
* Use a real potato or clay for the body	___/5
* Make body parts and accessories like hats, shoes, clothing, jewelry etc.	___/5
* Make 2 different sets of body parts and accessories	___/5
* Draw your potato people and label the body parts in English	___/5
Total points	___/25

Perform a Skit	
* "Visit" with a min. of 3 "patients"	___/5
* Neatly written or typed; give script for teacher to read before performance	___/5
* Use correct target vocabulary	___/5
* Include silly remedies or cures	___/5
* Perform for the class	___/5
Total points	___/25

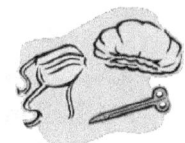

Cut Out Photos of Celebrities	
* 12 x 18 in.	___/5
* Use a min. of 5 photos	___/5
* Label a min. of 5 parts in each photo	___/5
* Use all target vocabulary words	___/5
* Include names of celebrities and give your work a title	___/5
Total points	___/25

Create a New Person	
* Min. 8.5 x 11 in.	___/5
* Label all parts using target vocabulary	___/5
* Include a brief bio of the new person	___/5
* Give the person a new name; include the name in the title of the work	___/5
* Write your name on the back	___/5
Total points	___/25

Differentiated Instruction for ESL Learners ©2013 Hubbert and Nieminen

Sports and Hobbies

Select two projects to complete.

Create a Commercial	Conduct a Survey	Make a Booklet
Make a commercial for your favorite sports team or hobby.	Survey your classmates in English to find out their favorite sports and/or hobbies. Make a graph based on your results.	Create a booklet with illustrations on how to play a particular sport or make a "how-to"-booklet for a hobby.
Make a Dictionary	**Your Choice!**	**Design a Game**
Create a dictionary in English in alphabetical order for a sport or hobby.		Make a game using either your favorite sport or hobby.
Create Trading Cards	**Give a Speech**	**Write a Biography**
Make a set of trading cards for your favorite sports figures or for important people in your favorite hobby.	Give a speech as you accept an MVP* award for a sport that you play or as you accept a trophy for your hobby. *Most Valuable Player	Write a bio about a sports celebrity in an English speaking country. Include a photo and bio information.

- **Challenge 1:** <u>Create an Instructional Video</u> on how to play a sport or how to do your hobby.
- **Challenge 2:** <u>Write an Original Theme Song</u> for your favorite sports team or hobby.

Create an Instructional Video		**Write an Original Theme Song**	
* 2-3 minutes long	___/5	* Min. 6 original lines in English	___/5
* Must be in English	___/5	* Song must include name of sports team or hobby	___/5
* Use good volume and clear pronunciation	___/5	* Must have a melody	___/5
* Give a copy of video for teacher to see before showing to the class	___/5	* Give copy of words or recording to teacher for review before performance	___/5
* Share video with the class	___/5	* Perform live or play recording to class	___/5
Total points	___/25	**Total points**	___/25

Sports and Hobbies Assessment Rubric

Create a Commercial		Conduct a Survey		Make a Booklet	
* Min. 1 minute long	___/5	* Survey a min. of 10 people	___/5	* 5.5 x 8.5 in., bound booklet	___/5
* Include a min. of 2 visual aids	___/5	* Give the graph an appropriate title	___/5	* Use complete sentences with correct grammar	___/5
* Slogan and all dialogue must be in English	___/5	* Label the axes	___/5	* Instructions clearly written in English	___/5
* Give script to teacher for review before performance	___/5	* Give original survey results to teacher	___/5	* Include color illustrations	___/5
* Perform live or play video to class	___/5	* Use color in the graph	___/5	* Cover must have title and student name	___/5
Total points	___/25	**Total points**	___/25	**Total Points**	___/25

Make a Dictionary		_____!		Design a Game	
* Min. 5.5 x 8.5 in., bound book	___/5		___/5	* Min. 20 question or activity cards in English	___/5
* Define a min. of 20 vocabulary words	___/5		___/5	* Use the name of your sport or hobby in the title	___/5
* Illustrations in color (drawings, magazine or internet pictures)	___/5		___/5	* Include a complete set of rules	___/5
* Must be in alphabetical order	___/5		___/5	* Must be in color	___/5
* Include title and student name on the cover	___/5		___/5	* Play the game; you are the leader of the game	___/5
Total points	___/25	**Total points**	___/25	**Total points**	___/25

Create Trading Cards		Give a Speech		Write a Biography	
* 3 x 5 in. index cards	___/5	* Min. 1 minute long	___/5	* 12 x 18 in. poster	___/5
* Make at least 10 cards, use English	___/5	* Give script for teacher to read before speech	___/5	* Include a color photo or an illustration of the person	___/5
* Include names and statistics of athletes or hobbyists	___/5	* Make the award or trophy that you are accepting	___/5	* Use English with correct grammar and spelling	___/5
* Illustration(s) in color (drawings, magazine or internet pictures)	___/5	* Deliver with good volume and excitement in English	___/5	* Bio must be factual	___/5
* Your name in lower left-hand corner of each card	___/5	* Quality of presentation is good (practice is evident)	___/5	* Present to the class	___/5
Total points	___/25	**Total points**	___/25	**Total points**	___/25

Show your project choices to your teacher by: _____

All of your projects are due on: _____

Feelings and Emotions

Choose two projects from the list to complete.

Use Feelings-and-Emotions Vocabulary in a Sentence
For example: We are_____ (happy). I am _____ (healthy).

Make a Poster
Illustrate and label feelings and emotions vocabulary on a poster. You may use magazine or internet pictures.

Create a Children's Book
Make a children's book with illustrations about feelings and emotions.

Make a List of Antonyms
List English antonym pairs (e.g. sad/happy) and then illustrate each pair.

Make Flip Books
Design 3 flip books with pictures on the front and English feelings or emotions vocabulary on the inside flap.

Make Greeting Cards
Create the following greeting cards: 1. Birthday for a boy, 2. Birthday for a girl, 3. Get well, 4. Thank you, and 5. Congratulations. Use English.

Make a Video for "Drama Class 101"
Videotape teachers or friends talking about feelings and emotions. Have each person act out two emotions or feelings. Describe their performances with a sentence in English.

Create a Collage Quiz
Make a collage to use as a quiz for feelings and emotions. Put the pictures on one side, and the target vocabulary on the other side.

Write a Story
Write a story using target emotions and feelings vocabulary.

Write a Diary or Journal Entry
Write down your emotions and feelings for one week. For each day, write out at least two sentences describing your emotions and feelings.

Feelings and Emotions Assessment Rubric

Use Vocabulary in a Sentence		Make a Poster	
* Write 10-15 sentences	/5	* Standard poster size	/5
* Use different subjects for each sentence	/5	* Include a min. of 20 illustrations	/5
* Must be complete sentences	/5	* Illustrate in color	/5
* Neatly written or typed	/5	* Label pictures in English	/5
* Use correct spelling and grammar	/5	* Give your poster a title	/5
Total points	/25	**Total points**	/25
Create a Children's Book		**Make a List of Antonyms**	
* Min. 5.5 x 8.5 in., bound book	/5	* Min. 10-15 antonym pairs	/5
* Min. of 10 pages with color illustrations	/5	* Use 5 of the pairs in sentences	/5
* Min. 10 target vocabulary expressions	/5	* Use correct grammar and spelling	/5
* Use correct grammar and spelling	/5	* Illustrate 5 of the antonym pairs	/5
* Write title and student name on cover page	/5	* Neatly written or typed	/5
Total points	/25	**Total points**	/25
Make Flip Books		**Make Greeting Cards**	
* Each book is 8.5 x 11 in., folded	/5	* Each card is a min. of 5.5 x 8.5 in.	/5
* Use 5 emotions per book	/5	* Include target vocabulary in the message	/5
* Illustrations in color	/5	* Neatly written or computer generated	/5
* Write a sentence on inside fold for each word	/5	* Illustrations in color	/5
* Underline the target word in each sentence	/5	* Trademark and student name on the back	/5
Total points	/25	**Total points**	/25
Make a Video for "Drama Class 101"		**Create a Collage Quiz**	
* Record 5 teachers or friends	/5	* 12 x 18 in. size collage	/5
* Write instructions for participants	/5	* Include 15 target vocabulary words	/5
* Have each teacher or friend perform 2 actions	/5	* All illustrations in color	/5
* Describe actions in English in the video	/5	* Neatly written or typed quiz on separate paper	/5
* Play video for the class	/5	* Answer key on reverse side of the quiz	/5
Total points	/25	**Total points**	/25
Write a Story		**Write a Diary or Journal Entry**	
* 1-3 paragraphs in English	/5	* Write daily entries in English	/5
* Use a min. of 10 target words in the story	/5	* Use journal or diary format	/5
* Must have a theme and a plot	/5	* Include date and day of week for every entry	/5
* Neatly written or typed	/5	* Write a min. of 2 sentences per day	/5
* Use correct spelling and grammar	/5	* Neatly written or typed	/5
Total points	/25	**Total points**	/25

Show your project choices to your teacher by: _____

All of your projects are due on: _____

Technology

Choose two projects to complete.

Send an E-mail

Send an e-mail to your teacher. Ask what are his or her favorite electronic items, movies, books, and hobbies.

Survey and Graph

Survey classmates in English about the technology items they own. Create an Excel spreadsheet and a graph.

Write Instructions for Internet Map Programs

Write simple instructions in English on how to use Google Maps or MapQuest.

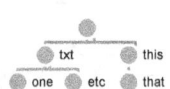

Research the Growth of Technology

Research the growth of technology in an English speaking country. Write an informational article or create a poster. May be computer generated.

Make a 3-D Museum Exhibit

Create an exhibit of early to modern communication devices in an English speaking country.

Make a Facebook Page

Create a Facebook page for inventors from an English speaking country who have improved technology.

Create a Cartoon

Create an original cartoon about technology or an electronic item. Choose still-life or animation for your cartoon.

Make a "Post-It" note Flipbook

Create a "Post-It" note flipbook about target country technology using target vocabulary.

Your Choice!

Technology Assessment Rubric

Send an E-mail	
* Subject line: Your name and class	____/5
* Ask 4 questions in English	____/5
* Use complete sentences	____/5
* Use correct spelling and grammar	____/5
* Last reply includes thank you to teacher	____/5
Total points	____/25

Survey and Graph	
* Survey 5-10 classmates	____/5
* Excel must be in proper format	____/5
* Create the graph from the Excel	____/5
* Use color in graph	____/5
* Share with the class	____/5
Total points	____/25

Write Instructions for Internet Map Programs	
* Write a min. of 5 steps or instructions	____/5
* Number each step	____/5
* Use English	____/5
* Computer generated with graphics	____/5
* Send electronically to teacher	____/5
Total points	____/25

Research the Growth of Technology	
* Include 3-5 methods of technology	____/5
* Min. 5 visuals or graphics	____/5
* Computer generated	____/5
* Give your article or poster a title	____/5
* Write your name immediately after the title	____/5
Total points	____/25

Make a 3-D Museum Exhibit	
* Must be 3-D	____/5
* Include a min. of ten 3-D objects in color	____/5
* Label each item in English	____/5
* Title must include name of the country	____/5
* Present to the class	____/5
Total points	____/25

Make a Facebook Page	
* Use Facebook template	____/5
* Include photo or illustration of inventor	____/5
* Include photo or illustration of invention	____/5
* Write brief description of invention	____/5
* Include bio of inventor	____/5
Total points	____/25

Create a Cartoon	
* Must be 6-8 frames and 8.5 x 11 in. if drawn, must be min. of 15 seconds if animated	____/5
* Must be in color	____/5
* All dialogue/words in English	____/5
* Each frame must include words	____/5
* Include title and student name in first frame	____/5
Total points	____/25

Make a "Post-It" note Flipbook	
* Include a min. of 25 post-it notes	____/5
* Use a min. of 5 vocabulary terms	____/5
* Use illustration on every page	____/5
* Flipbook has a clear theme	____/5
* Write title and student name on the front cover	____/5
Total points	____/25

_____!	
	____/5
	____/5
	____/5
	____/5
	____/5
Total points	____/25

Show your project choices to your teacher by:

_____

All of your projects are due on:

_____

Differentiated Instruction for ESL Learners ©2013 Hubbert and Nieminen

Unit 5: Score with Grammar

- **Teacher Tips for Pages 72 to 79** 73
- Nouns 74
- Adjectives 76
- Pronouns: Formal and Informal 78
- Verbs 80
- **Teacher Tips for Pages 81 to 84** 82
- Exclamations, Questions, and Declarative Sentences 83
- Likes and Dislikes 85

Teacher Tips for Pages 74 to 81

Standards

Nouns				Adjectives		
1.3 – 2W	1.3 – 2W	1.3 – 2W		1.3 – 2W	1.3 – 2W	1.3 – 2LS
1.3 – 2W	3.1 – 2LS +Tech	1.3 – 2LSW		1.1 – 2LS	1.2 – 2W	1.3 – 2W
1.3 – 2W	1.3 – 2RW	1.3 – 2LS		4.1 – 2W	1.3 – 2LS	
1.3 – 2W	1.3 – 2LSRW					

Pronouns: formal and informal				Verbs		
1.3 – 2W	1.3 – 2RW	1.3 – 2W		1.3 – 2W	1.3 – 2W	1.3 – 2W
1.3 – 2LSRW	3.1 – 2LSRW +ELA	1.3 – 2W		1.3 – 2LSRW	3.1 – 2RW +Art	3.1 – 2LS +Tech
1.3 – 2LSRW	1.3 – 2LSRW	3.1 – 2LSRW +ELA		3.1 – 2W +Art	1.3 – 2LSRW	1.3 – 2W
3.1 – 2LS +Music	1.3 – 2LSRW	3.2 – 2LS		1.3 – 2W	3.1 – 2LSRW +Drama	1.3 – 2LSRW

❖ **Preview Material**
   o For videotaped or recorded products, it is always wise to preview the video or recording prior to class presentation

❖ **Nouns**
   o For those students who choose "Be the Teacher," ensure that they are aware of time limits (that you set) as well as having all materials ready to be copied at least one day prior to the presentation.

❖ **Adjectives**
   o Ideas for "Your Choice": Create a song about all the colors of the rainbow. Write a poem using at least 15 adjectives on a subject of your choice.

❖ **Pronouns**
   o Review the elements of a well-developed paragraph prior to assigning projects.

❖ **Verbs**
   o See reference pages for *More Verb Activities* on page 116.

Easy Grading for *Score 100* menu:
This menu requires students to select one or more projects which add up to *Score 100*. To keep the assessment simple, the rubrics use the same point value (25) as the others. To calculate the final grade for each student, determine the percentage of points earned.
EXAMPLE 1: Student A has chosen the 20, 30, and 50 *Score 100*-projects from the menu. Student A has received 60 out of 75 on the assessment rubric. To determine overall percentage, divide 60 by 75. The student has earned an 80% for a grade.
EXAMPLE 2: Student B has chosen the 20 and 80 *Score 100*-projects and has received a total of 45 out of 50 on the assessment rubric. Divide 45 by 50; the student has earned a 90% for a grade.

Nouns

Score 100 ~ Gain yards with American Football
1. Select any combination of yards to total 100.
2. Mark your choices and show your teacher by: _____.
3. All projects are due by: _____.

20 Yard Run

Create a Brochure
- Make a brochure about nouns. Include 10 nouns and the rules of definite articles. Use English vocabulary.

Make a Store Sales Advertisement
- Create a store sales ad using the noun vocabulary with a minimum of 10 items. Pictures may be drawings, internet photos, or magazine cut-outs.

Construct a Mobile
- Build a mobile using the noun vocabulary and illustrations with 10-20 nouns.

Design a Collage
- Make a collage of noun vocabulary. Include answer key on the reverse side of collage.

30 Yard Field Goal

Make a Videotaped Commercial
- Make a videotaped commercial using noun vocabulary.

Create a Bingo Game
- Make a bingo game with the noun vocabulary. Include a minimum of 40 vocabulary words.

Make Themed Flashcards
- Make 2 sets of themed flashcards. Use one category of nouns: house, sports, clothing, food, etc.

50 Yard "Hail Mary"

Design a Crossword Puzzle and a Word Search
- Make a crossword puzzle and a word search for your classmates to solve using the noun vocabulary. May be computer generated.

Create a Class Activity or Game
- Make a class activity or a game to memorize noun vocabulary.

Make a Bulletin Board Display
- Design a bulletin board display titled "All About Nouns." Include pictures, labels, and descriptive sentences, etc.

100 Yard Touchdown

Be the Teacher
- Teach nouns to the class; include worksheet, visuals, homework assignment, and class activity.

Nouns Assessment Rubric

Create a Brochure		Make a Store Sales Ad		Construct a Mobile	
* 8.5 x 11 in., folded	/5	* Min. 8.5 x 11 in. ad	/5	* Include 10-20 nouns	/5
* Include 10 nouns with correct definite article	/5	* Include a min. of 10 items	/5	* Labels must be spelled correctly	/5
* Must have pictures and written information	/5	* Include sale and original prices	/5	* Include 2-3 hanging levels	/5
* Student name on the back	/5	* Each item must be in color	/5	* Illustrations in color	/5
* Neatly written and drawn or computer generated	/5	* Neatly written or computer generated	/5	* Must be balanced	/5
Total points	/25	**Total points**	/25	**Total Points**	/25

Design a Collage		Make a Videotaped Commercial		Create a Bingo Game	
* 12 x 18 in. collage	/5	* Min. 1 minute long	/5	* Set of 40 vocabulary cards, words neatly written	/5
* Write labels in English, spell them correctly	/5	* Include a min. of 10 items	/5	* Make 5 bingo cards using template	/5
* Name your collage	/5	* Use a min. of 1 visual aid per noun	/5	* Illustrations in color for each square	/5
* Select 20 themed nouns (e.g. clothing, food, school)	/5	* Include store name and slogan	/5	* Use correct spelling	/5
* Answer key with student name on the back	/5	* Pronounce words clearly	/5	* Pronounce clearly when leading the game	/5
Total points	/25	**Total points**	/25	**Total Points**	/25

Make Themed Flashcards		Design Puzzles		Create a Class Activity/Game	
* 3 x 5 in. index cards	/5	* Include 20 different nouns for each puzzle	/5	* All classmates must be able to play	/5
* Make 2 sets, min. 20 nouns for each set	/5	* Write appropriate clues for each puzzle	/5	* Write simple rules with an answer key	/5
* Use correct spelling	/5	* Include both puzzles and answer keys	/5	* Teacher must approve activity or game before play	/5
* Label on the reverse side of the color illustration	/5	* Your classmates must be able to solve the puzzles	/5	* Provide all required items for playing	/5
* Include container or bag for cards	/5	* Turn in solved and corrected puzzles to teacher	/5	* Lead the game or activity	/5
Total points	/25	**Total points**	/25	**Total points**	/25

Make a Bulletin Board		Be the Teacher	
* Min. 15 vocabulary words	/5	* Vocabulary list of 20 nouns	/5
* Be neat and creative	/5	* Fun class activity	/5
* Include colored illustrations and labels	/5	* Worksheet and visuals must be neat and creative	/5
* Include each noun in a complete sentence	/5	* Use correct grammar and spelling	/5
* Must be in English; use correct spelling	/5	* Include homework assignment and answer key	/5
Total points	/25	**Total points**	/25

Adjectives

Choose two projects to complete.

Find Adjectives

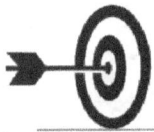

Find an adjective for each letter or character of the alphabet in English.

Illustrate Adjectives

Illustrate a min. of 10 adjectives and write a descriptive sentence for each.

Design an Award

Make an award for your best friend. Describe the award in detail with a min. of 10 adjectives using English.

Describe a Character

Describe a character from a book you are reading. Share your written description with the class.

Find New Adjectives

Use the dictionary to find 10 new adjectives and use them in sentences.

Create a Children's Book

Write and illustrate a children's book of adjectives; include colors.

Complete a Venn Diagram

Compare two items or people, e.g. cats/dogs, you/your brother, two friends, etc. Use English.

Describe a Teacher or a Friend

Describe your favorite teacher or best friend to the class. Use complete sentences in English.

Your Choice!

Adjectives Assessment Rubric

Find Adjectives		Illustrate Adjectives		Design an Award	
* Use 8.5 x 11 in. paper	/5	* Use 8.5 x 11 in. paper	/5	* Drawing or 3-D object	/5
* Illustrate a min. of 10 adjectives	/5	* Use English	/5	* 8.5 x 11 in. drawing, min. of 10 in. tall for 3-D	/5
* List in alphabetical order	/5	* Illustrate a min. of 10 adjectives	/5	* Describe award with a min. of 10 adjectives	/5
* Neatly written or computer generated	/5	* Use correct form of adjective in the sentence	/5	* Use adjectives correctly	/5
* Use correct spelling	/5	* Must be in color	/5	* Read description aloud to the class	/5
Total points	/ 25	Total points	/ 25	Total Points	/ 25
Describe a Character		**Find New Adjectives**		**Create a Children's Book**	
* Include a min. of 10 adjectives in the description	/5	* Min. 8.5 x 11 in. paper	/5	* Min. 5.5 x 8.5 in., bound book	/5
* Include photo or illustration of character	/5	* Include 10 new adjectives	/5	* Illustrate 10 pages in color	/5
* Include title of book and author in the description	/5	* Illustrate 5 in color	/5	* Use a min. of 10 adjectives	/5
* Neatly written or typed with correct grammar & spelling	/5	* Neatly written or computer generated in English	/5	* Neatly written or computer generated with correct grammar and spelling	/5
* Share with the class	/5	* Use correct sentence structure and spelling	/5	* Include student name on the title page	/5
Total points	/ 25	Total points	/ 25	Total points	/ 25
Complete a Venn Diagram		**Describe a Teacher or a Friend**		**_____!**	
* 8.5 x 11 in. paper	/5	* Min. 1 minute long	/5		/5
* Use two sets of comparisons	/5	* Give script for teacher to read before the speech	/5		/5
* Include a min. of 15 adjectives	/5	* Create the award or trophy in 3-D	/5		
* Use color and creative designs in the diagram	/5	* Deliver speech with good volume and excitement	/5		/5
* Title your Venn and label the sections	/5	* Great presentation (practice is evident)	/5		/5
Total points	/ 25	Total points	/ 25	Total points	/ 25

Show your project choices to your teacher by: _____

All of your projects are due on: _____

Pronouns

Score 100 ~ Qualify for Pole Position
1. Select any combination of laps to total 100.
2. Mark your choices and show your teacher by: _____.
3. All projects are due by: _____.

20 Laps

- **Make Flashcards** in the 1st, 2nd, and 3rd person singular and plural pronouns.
- **Make a Poster** containing all of the pronouns in English.
- **Design Greeting Cards:** one formal, one informal in English. Use a minimum of three different verbs.
- **Write 10 Sentences** using pronouns in English.

50 Laps

- **Write a Paragraph in English** about your family. Use a min. of 5-10 pronouns. Pronoun must correctly agree with noun and verb.
- **Design a Magazine Cover** with photos; use a min. of 5-10 pronouns in English on the cover.
- **Create a PowerPoint Game** using pronouns in English.

80 Laps

- **Create Three Dialogues** using informal and formal expressions to introduce friends and business colleagues.
- **Write a Paragraph in English** explaining informal and formal expressions in your native country.
- **Create a Song or a Rap** using all the pronouns in English.

100 Laps

- **Write a Skit about Pronouns** Include appropriate verb forms.
- **Conduct Two Interviews:** one formal and one informal. "Interview" the president or leader and a citizen of an English speaking country. Use English.

Pronouns Assessment Rubric

Make Flashcards		Make a Poster		Design Greeting Cards	
* 3 x 5 in. index cards	___/5	* Standard poster size	___/5	* Each card is 5.5 x 8.5 in.	___/5
* Include all singular and plural pronouns	___/5	* Neat and creative, written clearly in English	___/5	* Use pronouns and verbs correctly	___/5
* English on one side, your native language on the other	___/5	* Include all pronouns with correct spelling	___/5	* Neatly written and drawn or computer generated	___/5
* Include container or bag for cards	___/5	* Give your poster a title	___/5	* Trademark and student name on the back	___/5
* Play game with partner	___/5	* Use color	___/5	* Illustrations in color	___/5
Total points	___/25	**Total points**	___/25	**Total Points**	___/25

Write 10 Sentences		Write a Paragraph in English		Design a Magazine Cover	
* Number the sentences	___/5	* Min. 5-10 sentences	___/5	* 8.5 x 11 in.	___/5
* Use different pronouns and verbs	___/5	* Title your paragraph with your name below the title	___/5	* Include a min. of 5-10 pronouns in English	___/5
* Neatly written or typed	___/5	* Typed, double-spaced, max. size 14 font	___/5	* Include 5 photos or illustrations and a title	___/5
* Use correct spelling and grammar	___/5	* Pronouns, nouns, and verbs agree with each other	___/5	* Use correct spelling and grammar	___/5
* Read sentences to class	___/5	* Read to the class	___/5	* Must be in color	___/5
Total points	___/25	**Total points**	___/25	**Total Points**	___/25

Create a PowerPoint Game		Create Three Dialogues		Write a Paragraph in English	
* Min. 8-10 numbered slides	___/5	* Min. 3-4 lines per dialogue	___/5	* Min. 5-10 sentences	___/5
* Include all subject pronouns	___/5	* Correctly use pronouns in each dialogue	___/5	* Title your paragraph with your name below the title	___/5
* Write simple rules on separate slide	___/5	* Give copy for teacher to read before performance	___/5	* Include a min. of 2 informal and 2 formal expressions	___/5
* Include separate title slide	___/5	* Use correct spelling	___/5	* Read to the class	___/5
* Lead the game	___/5	* Perform with a classmate	___/5	* Neatly write or type with correct grammar & spelling	___/5
Total points	___/25	**Total points**	___/25	**Total points**	___/25

Create a Song or a Rap		Write a Skit about Pronouns		Conduct Two Interviews	
* 1-2 minutes long	___/5	* 3-5 minutes long in English	___/5	* "Interview" the president or leader of the target country	___/5
* Written words for teacher to read before performance	___/5	* Use all subject pronouns with correct verb forms	___/5	* "Interview" a citizen of the target country	___/5
* Must have a melody	___/5	* Give copy of script to teacher before performance	___/5	* Neatly write or type with correct grammar & spelling	___/5
* Include all pronouns	___/5	* Use correct and clear pronunciation during skit	___/5	* Write 10 questions for each person with answers	___/5
* Perform live or play recording to the class	___/5	* Perform for the class	___/5	* Perform interviews with a classmate for the class	___/5
Total points	___/25	**Total points**	___/25	**Total points**	___/25

Differentiated Instruction for ESL Learners ©2013 Hubbert and Nieminen

Verbs

Score 100 ~ Run, Jump or Throw for a Gold Medal
1. Select any combination of events to score 100.
2. Mark your choices and show your teacher by: _____.
3. All projects are due by: _____.

Discus 20

- **Make a Poster** of verbs by drawing or using magazine pictures.
- **Find Verbs in a Magazine or Newspaper** Find a current article in English and underline the verbs. Illustrate 5 of the verbs on a separate sheet.
- **Put Events in Order** Use verbs correctly to list the events of your gold medal party.

High Jump 30

- **Write 8 Sentences** to compare what you do and what your teacher does during the day. Use English.
- **Photograph Several People** *doing something*, and then label each photo with the correct verb in English.

Javelin 50

- **Videotape and Describe** friends and family doing different things. Include two different activities per person. Use target vocabulary.
- **Sculpt People or Animals** using clay or wire. Choose 10 verbs to sculpt. Write a sentence in English for each verb using "place card" labels.

Relay 80

- **Write a Commercial** to sell a product. E.g. exercise equipment, car, motorcycle, etc. Use English.
- **Write a Journal Entry** Write five entries for each day: yesterday, today, and tomorrow. Use correct verb tenses.
- **Write a "How To" Card** Try to use as many verbs as possible. The card can be for a fake item, but the item should be usable; e.g. "Alien catcher."

Marathon 100

- **Write and Act Out a Play** in English about verbs.
- **Be the Teacher** Teach verbs to the class; include visuals, a verb vocabulary list, a homework assignment, and a class activity.

Verbs Assessment Rubric

Make a Poster		Find Verbs in a Magazine or a Newspaper		Put Events in Order	
* Standard poster size	___/5	* Find a min. of 15 verbs	___/5	* Min. of 10 events	___/5
* Min. of 20 labeled verbs	___/5	* Underline all verbs	___/5	* Number the events	___/5
* Illustrations in color	___/5	* List verbs in alphabetical order	___/5	* Neatly written or typed in English	___/5
* Use English with correct spelling	___/5	* Write the definition for each verb in English	___/5	* Conjugate verbs correctly	___/5
* Give your poster a title	___/5	* Neatly written or typed	___/5	* Make invitation to the party	___/5
Total points	___/25	**Total points**	___/25	**Total Points**	___/25

Write 8 Sentences		Photograph Several People		Videotape and Describe	
* Use 10 action verbs	___/5	* Use 10 photos in display	___/5	* Min. 2 minutes long	___/5
* Number the 8 sentences	___/5	* Photos must be printed	___/5	* Include a min. of 10 verbs	___/5
* Conjugate verbs correctly	___/5	* Label each photo with correct verb in English	___/5	* Use correct pronunciation	___/5
* Neatly written or typed	___/5	* Use correct spelling	___/5	* Use complete sentences	___/5
* Read sentences to class	___/5	* Your display must be neat and creative	___/5	* Taping is of good quality	___/5
Total points	___/25	**Total points**	___/25	**Total Points**	___/25

Sculpt People or Animals		Write a Commercial		Write a Journal Entry	
* Use 10 verbs	___/5	* 30-60 seconds long	___/5	* Min. 15 entries in English	___/5
* Sculpture must be a min. 4 in. in height	___/5	* You must have the product to show in the commercial	___/5	* Neatly written or typed with correct spelling	___/5
* Use clay or wire in 3-D	___/5	* Give written dialogue to teacher before performance	___/5	* Include day and date for each entry	___/5
* Sentences must have correct verb structure	___/5	* Good volume and correct pronunciation	___/5	* Use complete sentences in 1st person	___/5
* Write sentences on "place card" labels	___/5	* Perform live or play video to class	___/5	* Use correct verb tenses	___/5
Total points	___/25	**Total points**	___/25	**Total Points**	___/25

Write a "How-To" Card		Write and Act Out a Play		Be the Teacher	
* Min. 5.5 x 8.5 in. card	___/5	* 1-2 minutes long	___/5	* Make a verb vocabulary list with 15 verbs	___/5
* Include a min. of 10 verbs with correct verb tense	___/5	* Use a min. of 15 verbs	___/5	* You must use supporting visuals	___/5
* The illustrations make the instructions clear	___/5	* Turn in the script to teacher before performance	___/5	* Include homework assignment and answer key	___/5
* The card provides clear instructions in English	___/5	* Include props and costumes	___/5	* Prepare well and be creative	___/5
* Number the steps	___/5	* Performance must be live	___/5	* Fun class activity	___/5
Total points	___/25	**Total points**	___/25	**Total Points**	___/25

Teacher Tips for Pages 83 to 84

Standards

Exclamations, Questions, and Declarative Sentences

1.3 – 2W	1.3 – 2W
3.1 – 2RW +Art	1.2 – 2LSRW
1.3 – 2RW +Tech	1.3 – 2RW
1.3 – 2LSRW	1.3 – 2LS
5.1 – 2LS	1.3 – 2W

Likes and Dislikes Page 1

1.1 - 2R	1.3 – 2LSRW	1.1 – 2W
1.3 – 2LS	1.1 – 2LSRW	1.3 – 2LSRW
1.1 – 2LSRW	1.3 – 2LS	1.3 – 2W

Likes and Dislikes Page 2

1.1 – 2LSW +ELA	1.1 – 2LSW	1.1 – 2LS
1.3 – 2W	1.3 – 2W	3.1 – 2LS +Music

❖ **Preview Material**
  o For videotaped or recorded products, it is always wise to preview the video or recording prior to class presentation.

❖ **Exclamations, Questions, and Declarative Sentences**
  o The *Ice-skating* column is lower level than the *Hockey* column.
  o In the assessment rubric, the assessment with *both* the skate and hockey skate apply to *Write True and False Sentences* and *Descriptive and Declarative Sentences*.
  o Options for extra projects:

  ♫ Using a "facial expressions chart," <u>Write Descriptive Remarks</u> using correct exclamatory sentences.

  ♫ <u>Make a Collage</u> of question words.

  ♫ <u>You Be the Teacher</u>; teach correct structure for simple declarative sentences.

  ♫ <u>Create a Chart</u> illustrating affirmative and negative sentences using appropriate sentence format.

  ♫ <u>Create a Quiz</u> about question words for your classmates to solve. Include an answer key.

  ♫ <u>Write 10 Statements</u> about a subject of your choice. E.g. family, friends, school, etc.

❖ **Likes and dislikes**
  o Due to the written and computer-generated content requirements, additional computer time may be necessary.
  o See page 2 or 73 for easy grading for *Score 100*-menu.

Exclamations, Questions, and Declarative Sentences

Skate around the Rink

1. Choose a total of three projects to complete from the *Ice Skating* and/or the *Hockey* columns.
2. One project needs to be chosen from each category in either column: Exclamations, questions, and declarative sentences.
3. Mark your choices and show your teacher by: _____.
4. All projects are due by: _____.

Ice Skating

Exclamations

- Make Flashcards using the target command vocabulary.
- Create a Children's Book using affirmative and negative sentences.

Questions

- Design a Poster of all the question words in English.
- Write Questions and Answers using all of the question words.

Declarative Sentences

- Make a PowerPoint describing your favorite places using pictures and statements.
- Write True and False Sentences about the culture of an English speaking country for a quiz.

Hockey

Exclamations

- Find 15 pictures in magazines and Write Descriptive Exclamations using complete sentences.
- Write 10 New Commands and instruct your classmates to do the commands.

Questions

- Create a Questionnaire and Interview a classmate or an English language speaker.
- Draw a Cartoon or a Comic Strip with a storyline using question words.

Declarative Sentences

- Write 10 Declarative Sentences using your current vocabulary list.
- Write True and False Sentences on a subject of your choice using English.

Exclamations, Questions, and Declarative Sentences Assessment Rubric

Make Flashcards		Create a Children's Book	
3 x 5 in. index cards	/5	5.5 x 8.5 in., bound book	/5
Include 15-20 commands	/5	10 pages with 1 sentence on each page	/5
Draw illustration on one side and write the English command on the other side	/5	Neatly drawn, written in English with correct spelling and grammar	/5
Include container or bag for cards	/5	Illustrations in color	/5
Play with a partner	/5	Include title and your name on cover page	/5
Total points	/25	**Total points**	/25

Design a Poster		Write Questions and Answers	
Standard poster size	/5	Number each question and answer	/5
Write a question using each question word	/5	Q & A must be complete sentences	/5
Include color illustration for each question	/5	Neatly written or typed in English	/5
Neatly written and drawn	/5	Must have correct spelling and grammar	/5
Title your poster and use correct spelling	/5	Present to the class	/5
Total points	/25	**Total points**	/25

Make a PowerPoint		Write True and False Sentences	
Make 10 content slides	/5	Write 10-15 T/F statements	/5
Color graphic(s) and words on each slide	/5	Use complete sentences	/5
Describe each place using English	/5	Use correct grammar and spelling	/5
Use adjectives correctly	/5	Type and number the statements	/5
Include your name on the title slide	/5	Include an answer key	/5
Total points	/25	**Total points**	/25

Write Exclamations or Declarative Sentences		Write 10 New Commands	
Write 10-15 sentences	/5	Write 10 commands in English	/5
Use correct spelling and grammar	/5	Classmates must be able to do commands	/5
Include a picture next to each statement	/5	Neatly written or typed	/5
Neatly written or typed in English	/5	Give copy to teacher before activity	/5
Read to the class	/5	Present to the class	/5
Total points	/25	**Total points**	/25

Create a Questionnaire and Interview		Draw a Cartoon or a Comic Strip	
Write 10 questions	/5	8.5 x 11 in. sized paper	/5
Give questionnaire for teacher to read	/5	Include 6 frames	/5
Neatly written or typed	/5	Write dialogue and/or text in each frame	/5
Write out Q & A in English	/5	All dialogue and text must be in English	/5
Read to the class	/5	Must be in color	/5
Total points	/25	**Total points**	/25

Differentiated Instruction for ESL Learners ©2013 Hubbert and Nieminen

Likes and Dislikes

Score 100 ~ Win Match Point with Volleyball
1. Select any combination of hits or passes to total 100.
2. Mark your choices and show your teacher by: _____.
3. All projects are due by: _____.

Serve for 20

- **List Five** of your likes and five of your dislikes. Use complete sentences.
- **Chart 10 Things** you like and/or do not like to do.
- **Make a Brochure** of your favorite and/or least favorite foods using target vocabulary.

Volley for 30

- **Videotape and Describe** 10 things you like and/or do not like to do.
- **Write to Express (A)** what your classmates like or dislike in the 3rd person singular using target vocabulary.
- **Write to Express (B)** what your classmates like to do or don't like to do in the 3rd person plural using target vocabulary.

Dig for 50

- **Survey Likes and Dislikes** of at least 10 classmates. Record on a poster.
- **Make a Wish Chart** using the phrase "I would like to..." in English.
- **Create a Scrapbook** of likes and dislikes using target vocabulary.

Spike for 80

- **Recommend a Book or a Movie** to a friend using the likes/dislikes vocabulary.
- **Present Your Point of View** using target vocabulary.
- **You Are the Judge** of a fashion show or cooking contest. Tell us your likes and/or dislikes.

Ace for 100

- **Invent a New Ice Cream Flavor** Tell everyone why your new flavor is the best.
- **Design a Magazine Cover** and create a full page advertisement on the back cover using the likes/dislikes vocabulary.
- **Write a Song** in English about likes and dislikes.

Differentiated Instruction for ESL Learners ©2013 Hubbert and Nieminen

Likes and Dislikes Assessment Rubric

List Five		Chart 10 Things		Make a Brochure	
* Include five likes	___/5	* Chart 10 likes/dislikes	___/5	* 8.5 x 11 in., folded	___/5
* Include five dislikes	___/5	* Illustrate 2-4 things	___/5	* Include a min. of 10 food items and illustrate in color	___/5
* Use complete sentences in English	___/5	* Use complete sentences, correct grammar in English	___/5	* Use correct grammar and spelling	___/5
* Neatly written or typed with correct spelling & grammar	___/5	* Neatly written or computer generated	___/5	* Include title and illustration on the front cover	___/5
* Illustrate each like and dislike	___/5	* Share with the class	___/5	* Neatly written and drawn or computer generated	___/5
Total points	___/25	**Total points**	___/25	**Total Points**	___/25

Videotape and Describe		Write to Express, (A) and (B)		Survey Likes and Dislikes	
* Include both likes and dislikes	___/5	* Include 10 typed sentences	___/5	* Standard poster size	___/5
* Narrate video in English	___/5	* Use correct grammar and spelling	___/5	* Survey 10 classmates in English	___/5
* Use complete sentences	___/5	* Use complete sentences	___/5	* Include both likes and dislikes	___/5
* Use clear volume and pronunciation	___/5	* Use 3rd person singular for (A), 3rd person plural for (B)	___/5	* Give your poster a title	___/5
* Share video with the class	___/5	* Read to the class	___/5	* Use color creatively	___/5
Total points	___/25	**Total points**	___/25	**Total points**	___/25

Make a Wish Chart		Create a Scrapbook	
* Include 10 wishes in your chart	___/5	* Min. 5.5 x 8.5 in., bound book	___/5
* Give copy of written phrases for teacher to read	___/5	* Include a min. of 10 pages	___/5
* Use color in the chart	___/5	* Include both likes and dislikes	___/5
* Give your chart a title and include a min. of 2 illustrations	___/5	* Illustrations in color (drawings, magazine or internet pictures)	___/5
* Present creatively to the class	___/5	* Title cover must have your name	___/5
Total points	___/25	**Total points**	___/25

Assessments continue on the next page

Likes and Dislikes Assessment Rubric

Recommend a Book or a Movie		Present Your Point of View		You are the Judge	
* 1-3 paragraphs, typed	/5	* Write 1-3 paragraphs	/5	* 10 likes and/or dislikes	/5
* Include name of book & author or movie & director	/5	* Title your paragraph(s) with your name below title	/5	* Use complete sentences in English	/5
* Use complete sentences, correct spelling and grammar	/5	* Use correct grammar and spelling	/5	* Make a creative display (e.g. poster, booklet, diorama)	/5
* Use a min. of 10 likes and/or dislikes	/5	* Use target vocabulary	/5	* Neatly written or computer generated	/5
* Present to the class	/5	* Read to the class	/5	* Share with the class	/5
Total points	/25	**Total points**	/25	**Total Points**	/25

Invent a New Ice-Cream Flavor		Design a Magazine Cover		Write a Song	
* Name the new flavor	/5	* Give your magazine a title	/5	* 1-2 minutes long	/5
* Write 1-3 paragraphs in English	/5	* Use likes and dislikes in layout and writing	/5	* Must have a melody	/5
* Use complete sentences, correct spelling and grammar	/5	* Graphics or illustrations must be in color	/5	* Use a min. of 15 vocabulary words	/5
* Include location (where people can buy it) and price	/5	* Neatly written and drawn or computer generated	/5	* Give written words for teacher to read before performance	/5
* Draw illustration(s) in color	/5	* Back cover ad must fill entire page	/5	* Perform live or play recording to the class	/5
Total points	/25	**Total points**	/25	**Total points**	/25

Unit 6: Going Places

- Teacher Tips for Pages 88 to 95 89
- Going to the Market 90
- Choose Your Ticket: Sporting Events, Concerts, Bus and Train Rides 92
- Vacation and Travel 94
- Visiting or Obtaining Services from Community Service Programs 96
- Teacher Tips for Pages 97 to 103 98
- Shopping Experience 99
- Eating Out 101
- Public and Private Schools 104

Teacher Tips for Pages 90 - 97

Standards

Going to the Market

4.1 – 2W	2.2 – 2W	1.3 – 5W
1.3 – 2W		2.1 – 1W
1.3 – 1RW	1.3 – 2LSWW	3.1 – 3LSW +Math

- Challenge 1: 1.3 – 2W
- Challenge 2: 2.2 – 2LS

Choose Your Ticket:
Sporting events, Concerts, Bus and Train rides

All Projects
4.2/Art/ELA – 2,5 LSRW

Vacation and Travel

2.1 – 5W	2.1 – 5LS	1.3 – 5W
1.3 – 5W	1.3 – 5W	3.1 – 5W +ELA
4.2 – 5W	4.2 – 5W	3.1 – 5LS +ELA

- Challenge 1: 3.2 – 5LS
- Challenge 2: 5.1 – 5W

Community Services Programs

3.1 – 5W +S.S.	1.1 – 2LS
4.2 – 5W	4.2 – 5W
3.2 – 1W	1.3 – 2LSW

❖ **Preview Material**
  o For videotaped or recorded products, it is always wise to preview the video or recording prior to class presentation.

❖ **Going to the Market**
  o If possible, purchase authentic food items from your local grocery store or online. Downloading photos and laminating the printed material would also be beneficial for student involvement.

❖ **Choose Your Ticket** is a Teacher's Choice. See page 2 or 36 for Teacher's Choice explanation.

❖ **Vacation and Travel**
  o Order travel brochures online or visit a travel agency and explore its selection.
  o Another version of "Choose Your Ticket": Set up a travel agency in your classroom. Students create dialogues to ask about travel destinations, purchase tickets, etc.

❖ **Community Service Programs** is a Teacher's Choice. See page 36 for Teacher's Choice explanation.
  o If possible, have copies of maps available for student use, especially city and state/province maps of the target country.

Going to the Market

Select "Three-in-a-Row" to complete the tic-tac-toe.

Describe Five Fruits and Five Vegetables	Illustrate a Cereal Box	Draw a Map
Describe five fruits and five vegetables using target vocabulary. Use a minimum of one adjective for each product.	Illustrate a cereal box from an English speaking country. Describe the cereal box with 2-3 sentences.	Draw a map of the grocery store or marketplace. Write descriptions of the aisles and products in English. 
Write a Grocery List	Your Choice! 	Make a Menu
Write a grocery list using target vocabulary.		Create a list of target country menu items for breakfast, lunch, and dinner. Use English.
Construct a Mobile	Write a Dialogue	Survey and Graph
Make a mobile of 10 food items with labels from an English speaking country. 	Write a dialogue for the market place; ask the clerk questions and include your answers. Use target vocabulary.	Survey your classmates about their favorite foods. Give them a minimum of five items to choose from and then graph the results.

- **Challenge 1:** <u>Write Out a Menu</u> in English for a birthday party using products found at the market.
- **Challenge 2:** <u>Create a 30-second Commercial</u> about a product you would find at the market. Use English.

Write Out a Menu		Create a 30-second Commercial	
* Make a shopping list of 20 products	___ / 5	* Min. 30 seconds long	___ / 5
* Include 5 menu items	___ / 5	* Include a slogan	___ / 5
* Illustrations in color	___ / 5	* Give the script for teacher to read before performance	___ / 5
* Include name of the party, date and time, etc.	___ / 5	* Include the product, prop(s), costume(s)	___ / 5
* Use a creative presentation format (e.g. poster, brochure, placemat)	___ / 5	* Perform live or play video to the class	___ / 5
Total points	___ / 25	**Total points**	___ / 25

Differentiated Instruction for ESL Learners ©2013 Hubbert and Nieminen

Going to the Market Assessment Rubric

Describe Five Fruits and Five Vegetables		Illustrate a Cereal Box		Draw a Map	
* Include 5 fruits	/5	* Approx. 9 x 11 x 2 in. box	/5	* 8.5 x 11 in.	/5
* Include 5 vegetables	/5	* Use English with correct spelling	/5	* Name the store	/5
* Use complete sentences	/5	* Must be in color	/5	* Include aisle labels	/5
* Use a min. of 1 adjective for each product	/5	* Include both words and illustrations	/5	* Use a map key to show locations of 5 products	/5
* Neatly written or typed with correct spelling & grammar	/5	* Use adjectives to describe product on the front cover	/5	* Use color	/5
Total points	/25	**Total points**	/25	**Total Points**	/25

Write a Grocery List		_____!		Make a Menu	
* 8.5 x 11 in. list	/5		/5	* Include 5 breakfast items	/5
* Include a min. of 20 items	/5		/5	* Include 5 lunch items	/5
* Use correct spelling	/5		/5	* Include 5 dinner items	/5
* Create an illustrated border around the list	/5		/5	* Use correct spelling	/5
* Neatly written or computer generated	/5		/5	* Include 1 illustration per meal	/5
Total points	/25	**Total points**	/25	**Total points**	/25

Construct a Mobile		Write a Dialogue		Survey and Graph	
* Include 10 food items	/5	* Min. 10 vocabulary words	/5	* Include min. 5 item choices	/5
* Label items correctly in English	/5	* Include a min. of 5 questions	/5	* Use English with correct spelling	/5
* Illustrations in color (drawings, magazine or internet pictures)	/5	* Include a min. of 5 responses using complete sentences	/5	* Title your graph and use correct graph format	/5
* Mobile must be balanced	/5	* Neatly written or typed	/5	* Use color in the graph	/5
* Display in classroom	/5	* Perform for the class	/5	* Turn in original tally sheet to the teacher with project	/5
Total points	/25	**Total points**	/25	**Total points**	/25

Show your project choices to your teacher by: _____

All of your projects are due on: _____

Differentiated Instruction for ESL Learners ©2013 Hubbert and Nieminen

Choose Your Ticket!
Sporting Events, Concerts, Bus and Train Rides
~ Teacher's Choice

Instructions:
1. Students are divided into 4 equal groups.
2. Groups: train, bus, concert, sports event.
3. Each student in a group will choose an activity to complete.
4. Paper money and coins will be made by each group.

How to play:
1. Choose one of the four settings and create stations.
2. One person at ticket counter with tickets and money.
3. 2-3 customers with money.
4. Students use appropriate dialogue to buy or sell tickets.

Make Tickets for Sporting Events
Create tickets for a sporting event. Prices need to be in target country currency. Use a variety of different prices. Name the sporting events, and include dates, and times.

Create a Program for a Sporting Event
1. 8.5 x 11 in., folded brochure
2. Illustrate front cover in color with title of event, date, and time
3. Neatly written and drawn or computer generated
4. Include list of events
5. Use target country sporting events

Make Tickets for Concerts
Create tickets for concerts. Prices need to be in target country currency. Use a variety of prices. Name the concerts, and include dates, and times.

Create a Program for a Concert
1. 8.5 x 11 in., folded brochure
2. Illustrate front cover in color with title of event, date, and time
3. Neatly written and drawn or computer generated
4. List of target country performers
5. Use English

Make Paper Money in the target country currency
1. Min. 5 x amount of maximum ticket price **
2. Large variety of denominations
3. Min. 50 bills in color
4. Target country currency
5. Cut out individually

** (e.g. ticket price=$10, you must make min. $50 worth of bills)

Make Coins in the target country currency
1. Min. 75 coins
2. Large variety of coins
3. Use cardboard or heavy paper
4. Use target country currency
5. Cut coins out individually

Make Train or Bus Tickets
Create tickets for the train or the bus. Prices need to be in target country currency. Use a variety of prices. Include the train and bus names, dates and times.

Create a Train or Bus Schedule
1. Each schedule: 8.5 x 11 in., folded
2. Include departures and destinations
3. Min. 1 graphic or illustration
4. Include times and days
5. Neatly written or computer generated

Choose Your Ticket Assessment Rubric
Sporting Events, Concerts, Bus and Train Rides

Make Tickets for Sporting Events		Make Paper Money in the target country currency		Create a Program for a Sporting Event	
* Prices must be in target country currency	/5	* Min. 50 bills in color	/5	* 8.5 x 11 in., folded brochure	/5
* Make a min. of 15 tickets	/5	* Use correct spelling	/5	* Illustrate front cover with title of event, date, and time	/5
* Use different prices	/5	* Use target country currency	/5	* Include list of events	/5
* Name of the sporting event must be on the ticket	/5	* Large variety of different amounts of money	/5	* Use target country sporting events	/5
* Dates and times in English	/5	* Cut out bills individually	/5	* Neatly written or computer generated	/5
Total points	/25	**Total points**	/25	**Total Points**	/25

Make Coins in the target country currency		Make Tickets for Concerts		Make Train or Bus Tickets	
* Make a min. of 75 coins	/5	* Make a min. of 15 tickets	/5	* Min. 15 tickets each	/5
* Target country currency	/5	* Prices must be in target country currency	/5	* Prices must be in target country currency	/5
* Make a large variety of coins	/5	* Use a variety of prices	/5	* Use a variety of prices	/5
* Use cardboard or heavy paper to make coins	/5	* Name of the concert must be on the ticket	/5	* Names of trains and busses must be on ticket	/5
* Cut coins out individually	/5	* Dates and times in English	/5	* Dates and times in English	/5
Total points	/25	**Total points**	/25	**Total points**	/25

Create a Program for a Concert		Create a Train or Bus Schedule	
* 8.5 x 11 in., folded brochure	/5	* Each schedule 8.5 x 11 in., folded schedule	/5
* Illustrate front cover in color with title of event, date, and time	/5	* Include departures and destinations	/5
* Include list of target country performers	/5	* Use a min. of 1 graphic or illustration	/5
* Use English	/5	* Include times and days	/5
* Neatly written and drawn or computer generated	/5	* Neatly written or computer generated	/5
Total points	/25	**Total points**	/25

Show your project choices to your teacher by: _____

All of your projects are due on: _____

Differentiated Instruction for ESL Learners © 2013 Hubbert and Nieminen

Vacation and Travel

Complete one from Column I and one more from Columns II or III.

Column I	Column II	Column III
Create a Diorama Pick a place to "visit" in an English speaking country and build a diorama.	**You are the Tour Guide** Pretend you are a tour guide in a major city in an English speaking country. Make a PowerPoint speech in English.	**Design a Brochure** Make a brochure for your travel destination in an English speaking country.
Create a Quiz and a Worksheet Make a quiz and a worksheet with vacation and travel vocabulary.	**Make a Pop-Up Book** Create a pop-up book of travel destinations in an English speaking country.	**Write an Article** Write an article for a travel magazine (e.g. NGS Traveler, Condé Nast, etc.) about a destination in an English speaking country.
Illustrate a Packing List Illustrate the items on a packing list as you pack for a trip to an English speaking country.	**Compare and Contrast** You are traveling to an English speaking country. Compare and contrast your packing list with that of someone traveling to your native country.	**Give a Persuasive Speech** Give a persuasive speech on the benefits of traveling to an English speaking country or city.

➢ **Challenge 1**: <u>Interview a Person from an English Speaking Country.</u> Find a person from an English speaking country and interview him or her about traveling to his or her homeland.

➢ **Challenge 2**: <u>Make a Complete Travel Schedule</u> for a two-week trip to an English speaking country. Include dates, days of the week, and a different activity for each day.

Interview a Person from an English Speaking Country		Make a Complete Travel Schedule	
* Include name, phone or e-mail address of the person for teacher to see	___/ 5	* Length of trip is two weeks	___/ 5
* Include a min. of 10 questions	___/ 5	* Include dates and days of the week	___/ 5
* Must be in English	___/ 5	* List a different site or activity for each day	___/ 5
* Videotape or record the interview	___/ 5	* Use complete sentences	___/ 5
* Share with the class	___/ 5	* Include transportation and places where you stay and sleep	___/ 5
Total points	___/ 25	**Total points**	___/ 25

Differentiated Instruction for ESL Learners ©2013 Hubbert and Nieminen

Vacation and Travel Assessment Rubric

Column I	Column II	Column III
Create a Diorama	**You are the Tour Guide**	**Design a Brochure**
* Min. 1 shoebox size (or approx. 5 x 14 x 16 in.) ___/5	* Make 10 content slides with correct spelling ___/5	* 8.5 x 11 in., folded brochure ___/5
* Include and label a min. of five 3-D objects ___/5	* Title slide must include your name ___/5	* Must contain facts and be written in English ___/5
* Decorate all surfaces ___/5	* Use graphic(s) and words on each slide ___/5	* Illustrations in color ___/5
* Give your diorama a title ___/5	* Write script out on separate sheet ___/5	* Use complete sentences with correct spelling ___/5
* Must be in English ___/5	* Present to the class ___/5	* Neatly written or computer generated ___/5
Total points ___/25	Total points ___/25	Total Points ___/25
Create a Quiz and a Worksheet	**Make a Pop-Up Book**	**Write an Article**
* Each sheet; 8.5 x 11 in. ___/5	* 5.5 x 8.5 in., bound book ___/5	* Write 2-3 paragraphs ___/5
* Use vacation and travel vocabulary ___/5	* Make a min. of 5 pop-up pages ___/5	* Typed, double-spaced, max. size 14 font ___/5
* Be creative and use color ___/5	* Must be in color and in English ___/5	* Location must be in an English speaking country ___/5
* Use correct spelling and grammar ___/5	* Illustrate front cover and include title and your name ___/5	* Photo(s) must be in color and must include caption(s) ___/5
* Include answer key ___/5	* Describe each location with complete sentences ___/5	* Use correct grammar and spelling ___/5
Total points ___/25	Total points ___/25	Total points ___/25
Illustrate a Packing List	**Compare and Contrast**	**Give a Persuasive Speech**
* 8.5 x 11 in. list ___/5	* Make a list for each person in English ___/5	* 1-2 minutes long ___/5
* Include a min. of 10 items in English ___/5	* Include a min. of 10 items for each person ___/5	* Must have persuasive elements ___/5
* Color each illustration ___/5	* Min. 2 illustrations per list ___/5	* Give typed script to teacher before presentation ___/5
* Include country name in the title of the list ___/5	* Compare in a Venn diagram or a paragraph ___/5	* Include a min. of 2 visual aids ___/5
* Neatly written or computer generated ___/5	* Label the Venn, title the paragraph ___/5	* Perform with clear volume and pronunciation ___/5
Total points ___/25	Total points ___/25	Total points ___/25

Show your project choices to your teacher by: _____

All of your projects are due on: _____

Differentiated Instruction for ESL Learners ©2013 Hubbert and Nieminen

Visiting or Obtaining Services from Community Service Programs ~ Teacher's Choice

Map Out the Embassy

Find out your home country embassy's address, phone number, and other contact information in an English speaking country. Draw a map from your "hotel" to the embassy.

Explain the Emergency

Pretend that no one can understand your native language, and that you must explain your problem to him or her in English. Choose 3:
- Injury (talk to the doctor)
- Toothache (talk to the dentist)
- Fire (talk to the fireman on the phone)
- Accident (talk to the police)
- Lost (ask a policeman for directions)

Compare and Contrast Professions

Compare and contrast professions between an English speaking country and your native country. Include the following:
- Training and Education
- Duties and Responsibilities
- Salaries
- Hours of work
- Vacation time

Compare Facilities

Compare medical facilities, police and fire stations, etc. in an English speaking country and in your native country.

Research Uniforms

Look for uniforms or attire for the following professions in an English speaking country:
- Doctor
- Dentist
- Police
- Fire

Display your work by using a PowerPoint presentation.

Write and Illustrate a Children's Book

Write and illustrate a children's book about going to the dentist or doctor or visiting a police or fire station in an English speaking country.

Visiting or Obtaining Services from Community Service Programs Assessment Rubric

Map Out the Embassy	
* Include address, phone number, and contact information for the embassy	____/5
* Include web page name and URL	____/5
* Pick a real hotel to "stay" at	____/5
* Map must be in color and must include a scale (e.g. 1 in. = 1 mile)	____/5
* Include map key and compass rose on map	____/5
Total points	____/25

Explain the Emergency	
* Write a min. of 4 sentences for each choice	____/5
* Use correct spelling and grammar	____/5
* Neatly written or typed in English	____/5
* Present to class with a partner	____/5
* Use correct pronunciation	____/5
Total points	____/25

Compare and Contrast Professions	
* 8.5 x 11 in. sheet for each profession	____/5
* Compare a min. of 3 professions	____/5
* Include separate paragraph or Venn for each, with separate titles for each profession	____/5
* Neatly written and/or drawn	____/5
* All required information is included	____/5
Total points	____/25

Compare Facilities	
* Select 3 facilities	____/5
* List 3 similarities and 3 differences per choice	____/5
* Min. 1 illustration per choice	____/5
* Must be in English with correct spelling	____/5
* Display your results creatively	____/5
Total points	____/25

Research Uniforms	
* Use 2 slides for each profession	____/5
* Each profession is included	____/5
* Graphics must be in color	____/5
* Write a short description for each uniform or attire using complete sentences	____/5
* Use correct spelling and grammar	____/5
Total points	____/25

Write and Illustrate a Children's Book	
* Min. 5 x7 in. bound book	____/5
* Min. 10 pages, must be in English	____/5
* Neatly written and drawn or computer generated with color illustrations	____/5
* Title your book and include your name on the front cover	____/5
* Read your book to the class	____/5
Total points	____/25

Show your project choices to your teacher by: _____

All of your projects are due on: _____

Differentiated Instruction for ESL Learners ©2013 Hubbert and Nieminen

Teacher Tips for Pages 99-105

Standards

Shopping		Eating Out			
All projects		All projects			
2.2 – **1, 2 W**		1.3 – **2, 5 LSW**	2.1	2.2	3.2

Public and Private Schools		
4.2 – 5W	1.3 – 5W	4.2 – 1W
4.2 – 5LS	3.1 – 2LS	1.3 – 2W
3.2 – 2W	1.3 – 2W	

- ❖ **Preview Material**
    - o For videotaped or recorded products, it is always wise to preview the video or recording prior to class presentation.
- ❖ **Shopping**
    - o If possible, take students on a field trip to an ethnic store in your area. Write out a pretend shopping list: assign students to find items in the store, have students find prices for certain items, and then compare online pricing of the same item.
    - o If not possible, go online to "shop".
- ❖ **Eating Out**
    - o Have students plan an ethnic dinner for the entire class. The students need to create a menu and a shopping list as well as dish assignments for each student group (e.g. Group 1 makes appetizers, group 2 makes the entrée, group 3 the dessert, and group 4 provides beverages).
    - o Take your student group to an ethnic restaurant.
- ❖ **Public and Private Schools**
    - o This is a Teacher's Choice. See page 2 or 36 for instructions on Teacher's Choice.
    - o Ask exchange students in your school to give presentations about their school systems.

Shopping Experience

Shopping Rules:
1. Choose a shopping experience.
2. Then choose a project to complete for that shopping experience.
3. Use English in all projects.
4. Show your choices to the teacher by:_____.
5. Your project(s) are due: _____.

Shopping Experience

- Clothing
- Personal Items
- Food
- Entertainment
- Sports/Fitness Equipment
- Hobbies
- Dishes
- School Supplies
- Music
- Automobile items or gas

Project

- Make a Scrapbook
- Write a Shopping List
- Design a Sales Ad
- Create a Poster or a Collage of Items from a Store

- Buy Holiday Items
- Create an Online Ad (e.g. E-bay, Amazon.com)
- Create the Front Page of an "Online" Store
- Draw a Map of Store Locations in an English speaking country or city

- Plan a Party
- Create an Advertisement
- Build a Diorama
- Draw a Store Front with Large Display Windows

Differentiated Instruction for ESL Learners ©2013 Hubbert and Nieminen

Shopping Experience Assessment Rubric

Make a Scrapbook		Buy Holiday Items		Plan a Party	
* Make a min. of 5 pages	/5	* Choose 10 items to "buy"	/5	* Make a shopping list of 10 items	/5
* Include a min. of 3 pictures in color on each page	/5	* Include prices for each item and label items	/5	* Party must have a theme (e.g. birthday)	/5
* Use correct spelling	/5	* Use correct spelling	/5	* Display cost of the party	/5
* Label pictures with prices	/5	*Display items creatively	/5	* Make an invitation	/5
* Include title and student name on front cover	/5	* Present to class in English	/5	* List 3 activities to do at the party	/5
Total points	/25	**Total points**	/25	**Total Points**	/25

Write a Shopping List		Create an Online Ad		Create an Advertisement	
* 8.5 x 11 in.	/5	* Include 5 items with prices	/5	* Standard poster size	/5
* Include 25 items	/5	* Must be in color	/5	* Must be in color	/5
* Include prices for all items with total cost	/5	* Use technology terms such as "add to cart"	/5	* Include slogan and price(s) for each item(s)	/5
* Neatly written or typed with correct spelling	/5	* Describe items with correct spelling and grammar	/5	* Write 5 sentences to describe each item	/5
* Include border or background for your list	/5	* Neatly written and typed or computer generated	/5	* Use correct spelling and grammar	/5
Total points	/25	**Total points**	/25	**Total Points**	/25

Design a Sales Ad		Create the Front Page		Build a Diorama	
* 8.5 x 11 in. ad	/5	* Include store name and catch phrase	/5	* Min. 1 shoebox size (or approx. 5 x 14 x 16)	/5
* Include a min. of 5 items with illustrations in color	/5	* Website format ; use tabs, e.g. sales, home page, etc.	/5	* Use store name as the title of the diorama	/5
* Include original and sale prices	/5	* Include "sale item of the week"	/5	* Must be an actual target country store	/5
* Use correct spelling	/5	* Must be in English with correct spelling & grammar	/5	* Use a min. of five 3-D objects	/5
* Include store name and date(s) of sale	/5	* Neatly written and drawn or computer generated	/5	* All surfaces must be decorated	/5
Total points	/25	**Total points**	/25	**Total points**	/25

Create a Poster or Collage		Draw a Map of Stores		Draw a Store Front	
* Standard poster size	/5	* Include min. 10 locations	/5	* 12 x 18 in.	/5
* Include a min. of 10 items	/5	* Use correct spelling	/5	* Include a min. of 15 items	/5
* Label each item (collage labels can be on the reverse side)	/5	* Label each location with store names and addresses (shopping center = 1 store)	/5	* Items in window can be photos, cut-outs, or drawings	/5
* Illustrations in color	/5	* Illustrate in color	/5	* Must be in color	/5
* Title your poster or collage	/5	* Include map key and compass	/5	* Store name must be from an English speaking country	/5
Total points	/25	**Total points**	/25	**Total points**	/25

Eating Out

Score 100 ~ Choose from the Buffet
1. Select any combination of buffet items to total 100.
2. Mark your choices and show your teacher by: _____.
3. All projects are due by: _____.

Appetizers 20

- Make a Crossword Puzzle with target vocabulary.
- Make a Reservation at two different restaurants.
- Write out a Recipe Card of menu items.
- Survey and Graph your classmates' favorite ethnic restaurants.

Beverages 30

- Identify Fast Food Restaurants in an English speaking country.
- Draw and Label a Floor Plan of a restaurant.
- Research a Restaurant from an English speaking country which serves foods native to that country.
- Your Choice!

Side Dishes 50

- Write and Perform a Skit about restaurants in a target country.
- Prepare a Dish from a real restaurant in a target country by researching their menus.
- Design a Placemat for a real restaurant in an English speaking country.
- Your Choice!

Entrees 80

- Videotape a Commercial for a restaurant in a target country.
- Design a Mural for a restaurant in an English speaking country.
- Write a Theme Song for a fast food restaurant.
- Your Choice!

Desserts 100

- Make a Board Game using restaurant and/or food vocabulary.
- Write a Critique in English of your favorite restaurant.
- Create a Pretend Website for your favorite restaurant.
- Your Choice!

Differentiated Instruction for ESL Learners ©2013 Hubbert and Nieminen

Eating Out Assessment Rubric

Make a Crossword Puzzle		Make a Reservation	
* Include 15-20 words	___/5	* Include 5 lines in English for each dialogue	___/5
* Write clear clues with correct spelling	___/5	* Neatly written or typed script	___/5
* Solution must be in English	___/5	* Use correct grammar and spelling	___/5
* Neatly written or computer generated	___/5	* Use correct pronunciation	___/5
* Include the answer key for the puzzle	___/5	* Perform with a partner to the class	___/5
Total points	___/25	**Total points**	___/25

Write Out a Recipe Card		Survey and Graph	
* Min. 5.5 x 8.5 in. card	___/5	* Survey 10 classmates	___/5
* Include name of the dish	___/5	* Ask questions in English	___/5
* Include list of ingredients	___/5	* Title your graph and label the axes	___/5
* Number each step of the recipe	___/5	* Graph must be in color	___/5
* Neatly written or typed with correct grammar	___/5	* Include original tally sheet	___/5
Total points	___/25	**Total points**	___/25

Identify Fast Food Restaurants		Draw and Label a Floor Plan	
* List names of restaurants	___/5	* Min. 8.5 x 11 in.	___/5
* Describe each restaurant in complete sentences with correct spelling	___/5	* Include all the important areas of a restaurant	___/5
* List the types of food served	___/5	* Use color	___/5
* Include some menu items with prices	___/5	* Label areas and items correctly in English	___/5
* Neatly written or typed in English	___/5	* Include a title for your work	___/5
Total points	___/25	**Total points**	___/25

Research a Restaurant		Write and Perform a Skit	
* Include name and location of restaurant	___/5	* 2-5 minutes in length, in English	___/5
* Include a min. of 10 items served	___/5	* Include a min. of 3 restaurants	___/5
* Use color	___/5	* Include props and costumes	___/5
* Display information creatively	___/5	* Give copy of written dialogue for teacher to read before performance	___/5
* Share information with class	___/5	* Perform skit with classmates	___/5
Total points	___/25	**Total points**	___/25

Prepare a Dish		Design a Placemat	
* Must be a real, native dish	___/5	* 12 x 18 in.	___/5
* Include the recipe	___/5	* Include the name of the restaurant	___/5
* Turn in your research	___/5	* Illustrations in color, must include border	___/5
* Photograph your dish	___/5	* Include both pictures and words	___/5
* Prepare dish and serve it to the class	___/5	* All words must be in English	___/5
Total points	___/25	**Total points**	___/25

Assessments continue on the next page

Eating Out Assessment Rubric

Videotape a Commercial		Design a Mural	
* 30-60 seconds long	___/5	* Min. 24 x 54 in. (= six 12 x 18 sheets of construction paper)	___/5
* Give script for teacher to read	___/5	* Include 15 illustrations	___/5
* Use good volume and clear pronunciation	___/5	* Neatly drawn or painted	___/5
* Include props and costume(s)	___/5	* Must be in color	___/5
* Perform live or play video for class	___/5	* Display in classroom	___/5
Total points	___/25	**Total points**	___/25

Write a Theme Song		Make a Board Game	
* 1-2 minutes long, use English	___/5	* Min. 11 x17 in. (an open file folder)	___/5
* Must have a melody	___/5	* 20 question or vocabulary cards in English	___/5
* Title your song	___/5	* Include title and background; must be food related	___/5
* Give written words for teacher to read before performance	___/5	* Must be in color	___/5
* Perform live or play recording	___/5	* Write a clear set of rules and directions	___/5
Total points	___/25	**Total points**	___/25

Write a Critique		Create a Pretend Website	
* Write 1-3 paragraphs	___/5	* Website format: tabs for menu & location, etc.	___/5
* Include food selection and service	___/5	* Make up a creative name and URL	___/5
* Give your critique a title and write your name below the title	___/5	* Neatly written and drawn or computer generated, use English	___/5
* Use correct spelling and grammar	___/5	* Include a min. of 3 graphics	___/5
* Must include one picture with caption	___/5	* Must be in color	___/5
Total points	___/25	**Total points**	___/25

_____!		_____!	
	___/5		___/5
	___/5		___/5
	___/5		___/5
	___/5		___/5
	___/5		___/5
Total points	___/25	**Total points**	___/25

Differentiated Instruction for ESL Learners ©2013 Hubbert and Nieminen

Public and Private Schools ~ Teacher's Choice

🎓 Write a Review about an English speaking country's school system. Include funding, classes, teachers, administration, etc.

🎓 Design a Brochure for a school or university in an English speaking country. May be fictional.

🎓 Fill out a Typical School Schedule for your grade level in an English speaking country. Use English.

🎓 Research High School Graduation Requirements in the target country and share your results creatively.

🎓 Produce a Videotaped Ad for a school in an English speaking country.

🎓 Draw a Storyboard illustrating "A Day in the Life of…" a middle school or high school student in the target country.

🎓 Make a Collage of classes, activities, logo, motto, etc. of a public or private school or a university in the target country.

🎓 Create a Pretend Facebook Page for a class, school, or university in the target country.

Public and Private Schools Assessment Rubric

Write a Review		Design a Brochure		Fill Out a Typical School Schedule	
* Write 1-3 paragraphs	___/5	* 8.5 x 11 in., folded	___/5	* 8.5 x 11 in.	___/5
* Typed, double-spaced, max. size 14 font	___/5	* Use both pictures and words (may be computer generated)	___/5	* Use table format, may be computer generated	___/5
* Use correct spelling and grammar	___/5	* Name of school and graphic on the front page	___/5	* Include all school days	___/5
* Min. 1 graphic with caption	___/5	* Include address and contact information	___/5	* Include all classes that are attended each day	___/5
* Include all required information	___/5	* Use correct spelling and grammar	___/5	* Include lunch and after-school clubs	___/5
Total points	___/25	**Total points**	___/25	**Total Points**	___/25

Research High School Graduation Requirements		Produce a Videotaped Ad		Draw a Storyboard	
* Include information about the graduation ceremony	___/5	* 1-2 minutes long	___/5	* 12 x 18 in.	___/5
* Discuss final or exit exams	___/5	* Include visual or item	___/5	* Min. 6-8 squares	___/5
* Include specific graduation requirements	___/5	* Turn in script for teacher to read before performance	___/5	* Include a picture with words in each square	___/5
* Display and share results creatively (e.g. poster, brochure)	___/5	* Use clear volume and correct pronunciation	___/5	* Include title and student name in the first square	___/5
* Present to class	___/5	* Present videotaped performance	___/5	* Illustrations in color	___/5
Total points	___/25	**Total points**	___/25	**Total points**	___/25

Make a Collage		Create a Pretend Facebook Page	
* 12 x 18 in.	___/5	* Include title for the page	___/5
* Include a min. of 10 items	___/5	* Use Facebook template	___/5
* Illustrations in color (drawings, magazine or internet pictures)	___/5	* Use complete sentences in the comments	___/5
* Include classes and activities	___/5	* Use English	___/5
* Include logo and motto	___/5	* Include a min. of 5 "posts"	___/5
Total points	___/25	**Total points**	___/25

Show your project choices to your teacher by: _____

All of your projects are due on: _____

Reference Pages and Templates

- ❖ Teacher Tips for Pages 108-116 107
- ❖ Shopping List 108
- ❖ Facts and Figures 109
- ❖ Commands 110
- ❖ Clock template 111
- ❖ Facebook Page template 112
- ❖ Race for the Numbers 114
- ❖ Bingo Chart template 115
- ❖ More Verb Activities 116

Teacher Tips for Pages 106-114

- ❖ **Shopping List**
  - Make copies, distribute to students and parents, and ask for donations.

- ❖ **Facts and Figures**
  - Copy the page for each student or group
  - Assign 5-10 items from the lists and choose the medium OR
  - Instruct student(s) to choose from lists: e.g. 5-10 items to display on a product of his/her choice
  - Have students create media products using all of the listed facts and figures

- ❖ **Commands**
  - Students never see the commands written. This is a Total Physical Response (TPR) activity. Students only hear and do the commands!
    1. The teacher must model each command when it is first introduced; students imitate the teacher.
    2. Only introduce two to four new commands each day.
    3. Previously learned commands should be reviewed daily for optimal student retention.

- ❖ **Clock template**
  - Tip: enlarge template before making copies

  Supplies you will need:
  - Two colors of construction paper, brass paper fasteners, glue, and scissors.
  - Use heavy paper or cardstock to copy clock face and hands, or have students glue onto construction paper. Cut out the hands.
  - Make a small hole in the center of the clock's face and one in each of the clock's hands. Using the brass paper fastener, attach the hands to the clock.

- ❖ **Facebook**
  - 1st empty space (rectangle): First Name
  - 2nd empty space (small square): Photo
  - 3rd empty space (rectangle): Full Name
  - Then fill in "Status" and "Comments"

- ❖ **Bingo Chart Template**
  - Students draw pictures of vocabulary words to use as bingo charts.

- ❖ **More Verb Activities**
  - A list of extra activities to use with verbs.

Shopping List

- Poster board
- Markers
- Colored pencils
- White copy paper
- 3 x 5 in. and 4 x 6 index cards
- 9 x 12 in. and 12 x 18 in. construction paper
- Scissors
- Old magazines
- Magazines in the target language
- Yarn/string
- Glue
- Tape
- Paper fasteners/brads
- Paper punch
- Rulers
-
-
-

Non-essential, but beneficial
- Magnetic strip
- Glitter glue
- Glue gun
-
-

Facts and Figures

The two lists below include the most common "facts and figures" categories for any target country that you are studying. To understand the culture and the language of a country, you should be familiar with the items on these lists. They are also an easy reference for you to make a poster of the target country's facts and figures.

- Currency
- Population
- Language(s) spoken
- Capital and major cities
- History and historical dates
- Types of ethnicities/holidays/celebrations
- Principal products
- Natural resources
- Economy: agriculture and industry
- Imports and exports
- Geography and physical features
- Making a living/median wage
- Foods
- Government

- Nature: animals and plants
- Climate: seasons and weather
- Places of interest and historical sites
- Sports: national and international
- Transportation
- Education: public and private
- Map: outline, latitude, longitude
- Military: types and service
- National flag, anthem, motto, symbols, crest, etc.
- Communication and technology
- Religion(s)
- Family life

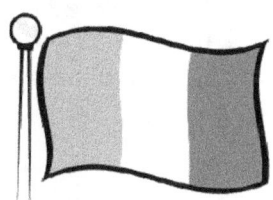

Commands

1. Stand up. Sit down.
2. Raise your right hand.
3. Raise your left hand.
4. Put your hands over your head, over the book, pencil, stapler, etc.
5. Touch your nose.
6. Touch the desk.
7. Touch the floor.
8. Touch another person's desk.
9. Touch the board.
10. Touch the teacher's desk.
11. Open the door.
12. Close the door.
13. Open the window, curtain, cupboard, etc.
14. Close the window, curtain, cupboard, etc.
15. Turn on the lights.
16. Turn off the lights.
17. Sit down.
18. Sit in another chair/desk.
19. Sit in the teacher's chair.
20. Sit on the floor.
21. Come here.
22. Put your pencil on the floor.
23. Pick up the pencil on the floor.
24. Turn around.
25. Turn to the right.
26. Turn to the left.
27. Trade seats with another person.
28. Trade pencils with another person.
29. Trade books with another person.
30. Throw away paper.
31. Write your name on the board.
32. Write the numbers 1-10 on the board.
33. Draw a big circle on the board.
34. Draw a house in the circle.
35. Draw a tree in the circle.
36. Erase the board.
37. Erase the house in the circle.
38. Shake hands with another person/teacher.
39. Bark like a dog.
40. Shout "Look at me!"
41. Walk around your desk, the teacher's desk.
42. Jump up and down.
43. Jump over the paper on the floor.
44. Say "hi" to another person.
45. Tell me your birthday.
46. Make a basket. (Nerf ball and net) ☺
47. Bring me your pencil.
48. Walk to the teacher's desk.
49. Write "THE" on the board.
50. Write "END" on the board.

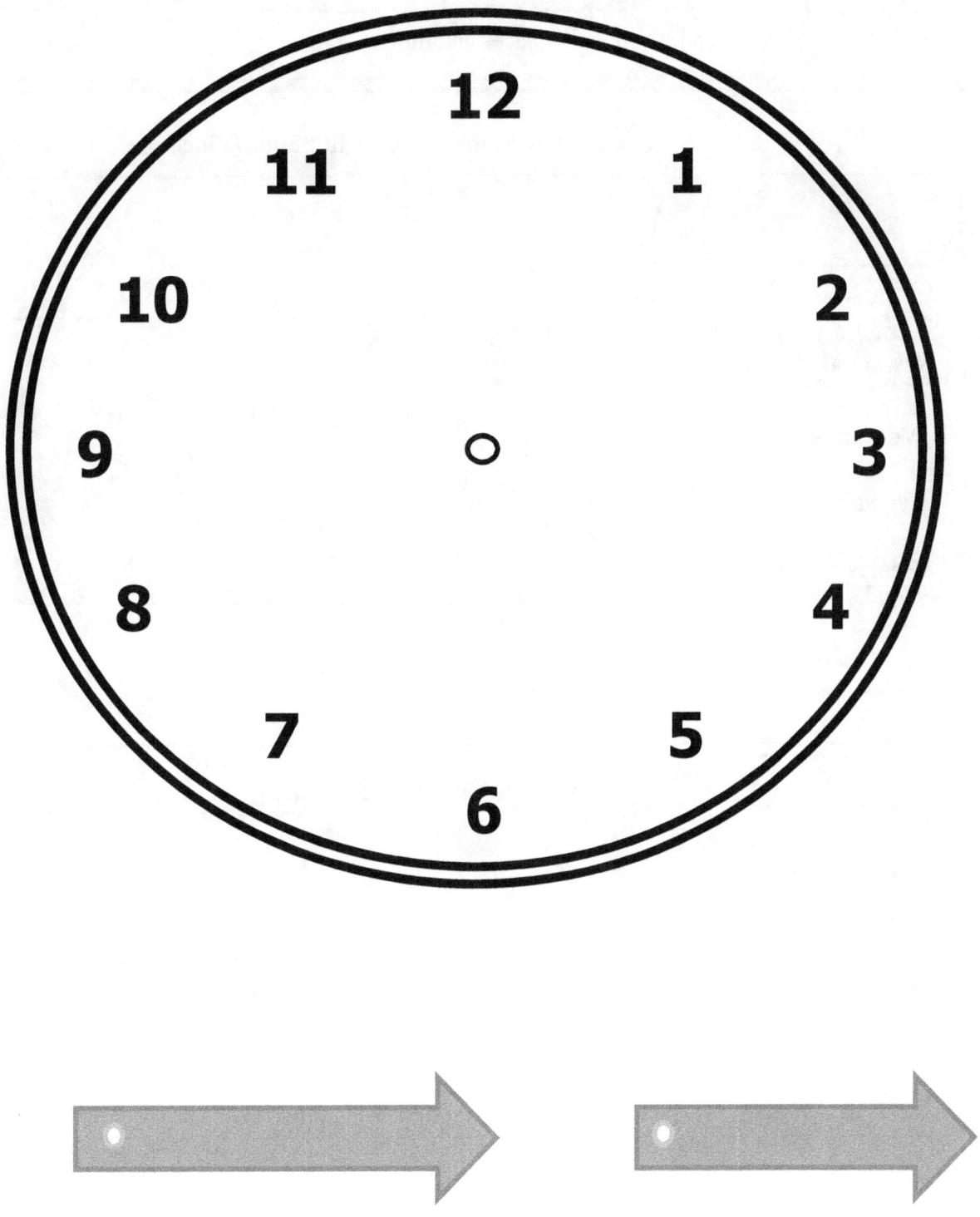

- o   Glue onto construction paper. Cut out the hands.
- o   Make a small hole in the center of the clock's face and one in each of the clock's hands.
- o   Using the brass paper fastener, attach the hands to the clock.

facebook   Search for people, places and thing 🔍   Home

Update Status   **Add Photos/Video**

Newsfeed

Messages

Events

Photos

Groups

Apps

Like · Comment · Share ·

Like · Comment · Share ·

Like · Comment · Share ·

112

Differentiated Instruction for ESL Learners   ©2013 Hubbert and Nieminen

☐ Update Status 　Add Photos/Video

Like · Comment · Share ·

Like · Comment · Share ·

Like · Comment · Share ·

Race for the Numbers

Instructions for the Game:

The object of the game is to see who can identify the selected number on the board the fastest.

1. Arabic numerals 1-100 are written randomly on the white-board with a black marker.
2. The class is divided into two teams. Each team is assigned a "color" by the teacher depending on the color availability of the marker selection. ☺
3. Choose one person to be the "fixer." This person's job is to erase any incorrectly circled number and to re-write the number in its original form. Reminder: The fixer uses a black marker!
4. The teacher calls out a number in English.
5. One person from each team races to the board to find the number. When they find it, they must circle it with a marker. (Each team *must* use their assigned colored marker to circle the numbers!)
6. If the wrong number is circled, continue play until the *correct* number is circled.
7. However, if neither player circles the *correct* number within a teacher-determined time limit, the number is discarded.
8. The winning team is the one that has identified the most numbers *correctly*.

Timesaving Teacher Tips:

- ❖ Teacher selects team captains who then select their teams. Each captain assigns playing order for team members (first, second, third, etc.)

- ❖ Make (or have students make) a set of cards with numbers 1-100. Use those numbers to select from - this also ensures that each number is only called once. You can also use the cards to keep track of scoring in the following way:
  1. Assign colors for the teams based on your marker-color selection as mentioned above.
  2. Lay corresponding pieces of colored construction paper on either side of you.
  3. When a team gets a point, lay the number on its corresponding colored paper.

- ❖ Instead of having to write the numbers on the board each time you play the game, write the numbers on index cards, laminate them, and then affix a short strip of magnetic tape on the back. Students can then identify the numbers by drawing an X or / on the card with their marker.

By Sue Hubbert

More Verb Activities

- Make flashcards of verb vocabulary.
- Make a flipbook using verb vocabulary.
- Draw a cartoon/comic using verbs vocabulary.
- Create a word search with target vocabulary.
- Create a children's book of verbs.
- Write simple sentences about professions using action verbs.
- Make a scrapbook of 15 verbs using different tenses.
- Make a game of commands using verb vocabulary.
- Survey classmates about their weekend activities; translate their answers into English or use English throughout survey.
- Create a crossword puzzle where the solution word is a verb.
- Choose a famous person to role play from the target country. Describe 10 activities you can/would do if you were that person.

Notes:

www.ingramcontent.com/pod-product-compliance
Lightning Source LLC
Chambersburg PA
CBHW081422230426
43668CB00016B/2322